LINGUISTICS
AND
BILINGUAL DICTIONARIES

LINGUISTICS
AND
BILINGUAL DICTIONARIES

BY

ALI M. AL-KASIMI

University of Riyadh

LEIDEN
E. J. BRILL
1977

To Archibald A. Hill

TABLE OF CONTENTS

PREFACE

As a result of the flourishing increase in international interaction and cooperation, more and more of us are coming to realize that bilingual dictionaries have become a necessary part of our daily economic, intellectual, and cultural activities. Bilingual dictionaries in current use have grown out of practice and tradition rather than scientific research and can no longer meet our needs. This book gives an account of the linguistic principles that should govern the production of better bilingual dictionaries and is intended for linguists, lexicographers, librarians, and foreign language teachers. It gives linguists an insight into the practical problems of compiling dictionaries, acquaints lexicographers with the theoretical approaches to the linguistic problems they encounter in their careers, provides librarians with a new system of classifying bilingual dictionaries, and helps language teachers to select the most appropriate dictionaries for their students.

I am indebted to my professor Dr. Archibald A. Hill, whose publications, courses, discussions, and library have given great impetus to my linguistic education. I am also grateful to Professor James Sledd, with whom I studied lexicography. I owe many thanks to Drs. Peter Abboud, Najim Bezirgan, John Bordie, A. A. Fedda, William Herold, Ezzat Khattab, Joseph Michel, and Mark Seng; their directions and suggestions have been most valuable to me throughout my study and work at the University of Texas and the University of Riyadh. Special thanks go to the University of Texas Graduate School for their financial support of the research on this book and to the University of Riyadh for subsidizing its publication.

A.M.K.

CHAPTER ONE

INTRODUCTION

LINGUISTICS AND LEXICOGRAPHY

1.1 *The Statement of the Problem*

In linguistic terminology, a distinction is made between "lexicology" and "lexicography." The former refers to the study of words and their meanings in one language or a group of languages. The latter designates the making of dictionaries. Basically, lexicology is concerned with the lexical systems of the language such as sememic syntax, sememic components, idioms, synonymy, polysemy, and lexemic components.[1] As for dictionary making, it involves five principal steps: gathering of data, parsing and excerpting of entries, filing of entries according to a certain arrangement, writing of articles, and publication of the final product.[2] The finished product is the dictionary which can be defined as "a book containing a selection of words, usually arranged alphabetically, with explanations of their meanings and other information concerning them, expressed in the same or another language."[3] It is, therefore, obvious that lexicography is dependent on, but not the same as, lexicology.

Dictionaries have developed not as theoretical instruments, but as practical tools. The major motives behind the rise of lexicography differ from one culture to another. Each culture fosters the development of dictionaries appropriate to its characteristic demands. The oldest existing dictionaries were made in Iraq for practical reasons; the Assyrians who came to Babylonia about three thousand years ago had difficulty in understanding the Sumerian signs, and their schoolboys found it useful to prepare "syllabaries" giving the Sumerian

---

[1] Sydney M. Lamb, "Lexicology and semantics," in *Linguistics Today*, ed. by Archibald A. Hill (New York: Basic Books, Inc., 1969), pp. 40-49.

[2] I. J. Gelb, "Lexicography, lexicology, and the Accadian dictionary," in *A. Andre Martinet E structuralismo e Historia II.* (Canarias: Universidad de la Laguna, 1958), p. 66.

[3] C. L. Barnhart, *The American College Dictionary* (New York: Random House, 1966).

signs and their Assyrian translations.[4] Arabic lexicography emerged in the seventh century for religious reasons; dictionaries were first written to explain the rare words which occurred in the Koran and Hadith.[5] The first English bilingual glossaries evolved to meet educational needs; the schoolmasters compiled those Latin-English glossaries to help their pupils understand the textbooks which were written in Latin.[6] American lexicography was encouraged by nationalistic zeal;[7] Noah Webster's dictionaries "were suggested partly by his resentment against the ignorance concerning American institutions shown in contemporary British dictionaries."[8]

This practical orientation of dictionaries contributed to the creation and growth of a gap between linguistic theory and lexicographical practice. Although modern linguists have done a great deal in the scientific study of language, lexicographers did not make much use of the linguistic findings in their dictionaries. As late as 1963, Marckwardt complained of the lack of application of linguistic principles in the English dictionary :

> Structural concepts do not appear with any great frequency in the dictionary. Words are traditionally classified as nouns, adjectives, verbs, and so on. There was no attempt to substitute a scheme consistently based either upon form or function. This is a dictionary of words rather than of morphemes. I find it difficult to detect even a hint of structuralism in the handling of definitions.[9]

Another linguist, Weinreich, noted that *Webster's Third*, which is one of the finest dictionaries ever produced in the English speaking world, lacks a sound theoretical basis :

> It is disconcerting that a mountain of lexicographic practice such as an unabridged dictionary of English should yield no more than a paragraph-sized molehill of lexicological theory.[10]

---

[4] C. F. Jean, *La Littérature des Babyloniens et des Assyriens* (Paris, 1924), p. 281 ff., summarized in John Haywood, *Arabic Lexicography* (Leiden : E. J. Brill, 1960), p. 5.

[5] Hussein Naṣṣār, *Al-Mu'jam Al-'arabi* (Cairo : Dāru'l-Kātib, 1956), pp. 39-66.

[6] James A. Murray, *The Evolution of English Lexicography* (Oxford, 1900), pp. 7-9.

[7] Joseph H. Friend, *The Development of American Lexicography 1798-1864* (The Hague : Mouton, 1967), p. 9.

[8] Philip B. Gove, ed., *Webster's Third New International Dictionary* (Springfield, Mass. : G. & C. Merriam Co., 1969), Noah Webster's Biography.

[9] Albert H. Marckwardt, "Dictionaries and the English language," *English Journal*, 52 (1963), p. 344.

[10] Uriel Weinreich, "Webster's Third : A critique of its semantics," *International Journal of American Linguistics*, 30 (1964), p. 408.

On the other hand, lexicographers claim that lexicography is not a scientific activity but an art which cannot abide by the objective methodology of modern linguistics. In the words of Gove :

> Lexicography is not yet a science. It may never be. It is an intricate and subtle and sometimes over-powering art, requiring subjective analysis, arbitrary decisions, and intuitive reasoning.[11]

The major factors that contributed to the widening of the gap between linguistic theory and lexicographic practice can be summarized as follows :

(a) For a long time in the history of English lexicography no serious thought had ever been given to treating the methodology of lexicography on a general theoretical basis. Dictionaries just grew, guided by convenience and convention, and were most of the time commercial undertakings rather than scholarly achievements. The best commercial dictionary would aspire "to answer the questions that the user of the dictionary asks"[12] as Barnhart said, not to extend "far beyond the first expectation of the purchasers..."[13] as Coleridge wanted it to do. Lexicographers did not make a sincere effort to acquaint themselves with linguistic theories and apply them in their dictionaries. In 1934, Mansion noted that "bilingual dictionaries are not scientific in their treatment of words, and have not kept pace with progress in philology that has been so notable in recent years," and added that "the mind of the lexicographer seems invariably to be anchored in the past..."[14] Mansion's remark is still true to a large extent. Commercial lexicographers do not pay much attention to modern advances in linguistics. To do this is expensive and time-consuming; besides they might take the risk of losing their audience. The contradiction between linguistic methodology and the conventional expectations of the public is noticed by Read who said :

> There is a constant pulling and hauling between what a lexicographer would like to do on scientific grounds, and what he is compelled to do by the habitual demands of the public.[15]

---

[11] Philip B. Gove, "The dictionary's function," in *The Role of the Dictionary*, ed. by Philip B. Gove (Indianapolis : The Bobbs-Merrill Co., Inc., 1967), p. 7.

[12] C. L. Barnhart, "Problems in editing commercial monolingual dictionaries," in *Householder and Saporta*, p. 161.

[13] S. T. Coleridge, *Treatise on Method*, ed. by Alice D. Snyder (London : Constable & Co., Ltd., 1934), p. 74.

14 J. E. Mansion, ed. *Harrap's Standard French and English Dictionary*, Part 1 (London : George G. Harrap and Co., Ltd., 1934) ed. 1958, p. v.

[15] Allen Walker Read, "Approaches to lexicography and semantics," in *Modern Trends in Linguistics 10*, ed. by Thomas Sebeok (The Hague : Mouton, 1972), p. 619.

(b) Modern American linguists in the twentieth century have neglected the lexicon for other interests. The Bloomfieldian school, which dominated the linguistic stage in the U.S. until the last decade, looked at the lexicon (dictionary) as "an appendix of grammar, a list of basic irregularities,"[16] and subsequently the leaders of the new science neglected it for more regular aspects of the language. In the words of Gleason :

> Certainly we descriptive linguists tend to be contemptuous of vocabulary. It is almost a dogma among us that vocabulary is the least significant part of language (save for a group among us who even doubt that vocabulary is really a part of language after all.)[17]

(c) The eternal problem that confronts theorists is the impracticality of their theories. Hill rightly noted that "current linguistic practice is so heavily weighted toward theory," and reminded us that "theory is a sword which scholars have not merely lived by, but perished by as well."[18] Urdang admits the importance of linguistic theories for the lexicographer, but he reminds linguists that their theories should have practical feasibility :

> Lexicography, in practice is a form of applied linguistics and, although more theoreticians would be a welcome addition to the field, they must remember that their theories should be interpretable above all in terms of practicality.[19]

The situation will not be improved until lexicographers learn at least something about what the theorists say, and until theorists have some familiarity with the relevant data.[20] With justification, Hall pointed out that some of the best linguistic theories intended as an aid to develop lexicographical methodology are "unrealistic demands for unreasonable and unworkable detail."[21]

(d) Even if a lexicographer was willing to accommodate linguistic principles in his work, he would face two major problems :

---

[16] Leonard Bloomfield, *Language* (New York : Holt, Rinehart and Winston, 1933), p. 274.

[17] H. A. Gleason, Jr., "The relation of lexicon and grammar," in Householder and Saporta, p. 86.

[18] Archibald A. Hill, "Review of an introduction to general linguistics by Francis P. Dineen," *Lingua*, 22 (1969), p. 238.

[19] Laurence Urdang, "Review of Problems in Lexicography," *Language*, 39 (1963), p. 594.

[20] James Sledd, Lectures on Lexicography at the University of Texas, Fall 1971, taped by the writer.

[21] Robert A. Hall, Jr., "Some recent developments in American linguistics." *Neuphilologische Mitteilungen*, 70 (1969), p. 215.

(1) The rapid change in the linguistic scene. During the last two decades alone, the U.S. witnessed the emergence of a number of linguistic theories such as transformational, tagmemic, stratificational, in addition to the structural theory. Compiling and editing a scholarly dictionary might take ten years or more. A lexicographer might find the linguistic theory on which he based his work obsolete and old-fashioned before his dictionary was published.

(2) Even within one school of thought, different linguists deal with the same problem differently. Let us look at Marckwardt's criticism regarding the lexicographers' traditional classifications of words as nouns, adjectives, verbs and so on (P.2), and see how structural linguists to whom he belongs deal with the problem. As is indicated in the table designed by MacKey, various classifications of parts of speech show perplexing diversity. Jespersen has only 6 parts of speech; Fries gives nineteen. Some of the differences reflect different approaches or different bases of classification.[22] In this case, the lexicographer is in a critical situation, and the only safe guides he can perceive are convenience and convention. But Mackwardt is right in demanding that dictionaries should adopt a consistent objective criterion for their classifications of words into parts of speech according either to form or to function.

1.2 *The Need for the Study*

The neglect of lexicography by American linguists is beginning to come to an end. During the last decade there has been a great deal of urging to integrate semantics in the linguistic description and theory. Consequently lexicography has been given a new impetus and has become closer to the center. Attention given to lexicography has been shown in a series of events, a sample of which follows :

(a) In 1960, a group of linguists and lexicographers held a conference at Indiana University to discuss a variety of problems related to lexicography. Their papers were collected and published in book form which received a good deal of attention.[23]

---

[22] H.A. Gleason, Jr., *Linguistics and English Grammar.* (New York : Holt, Rinehart and Winston, Inc., 1965), p. 125.

[23] Fred W. Householder and Sol Saporta, eds., *Problems in Lexicography.* (Bloomington : Indiana Univ., 1967), 286 pp.

TRADITIONAL	SWEET	SLEDD Morphological	SLEDD Syntactic Minor	SLEDD Syntactic Major	JESPERSEN Ranks	JESPERSEN Parts of Speech	ROBERTS Form Classes	ROBERTS Structure Words	FRIES Form Classes	FRIES Function Word Groups	HILL
article	Declinable		determiner					determiners		A	
pronoun	noun†	pronoun	reflexive	nominals	primaries	pronouns++		pronouns	1		pronouns
noun	noun†	noun		nominals	primaries	nouns*	noun		1		nouns
adjective	adjective°	adjective		adjectivals	secondaries		adjective		3		adjectives
verb	verb	verb		auxiliary verbals	secondaries	verbs	verb	auxiliary verbs	2	B / G	verbs
adverb	Undeclinable: adverb	adverb	adverbs of degree	adverbials	tertiaries	particles	adverb	intensifiers	4	C / D / H / I	adverbs
			interrogative adverbs					question words			
preposition	preposition		preposition					prepositions		F	prepositions
conjunction	conjunction		conjunction					conjunctions		E	conjunctions
								sentence connectors		J	
								subordinates		K / L / M / N / O	
interjection	interjection							etc.			

* includes adjectives   † includes pronouns   ‡ includes articles   o includes participles

Table 1: English Parts of Speech in the Twentieth Century (From MacKey's Language Teaching Analysis, pp. 66 & 67)

(b) The publication of *Webster's Third* in 1961 raised a storm of criticism and comments. Numerous linguists, lexicographers, educators, and journalists took part in the debate. Sledd and Ebbitt's *Dictionaries and That Dictionary* includes 62 articles which appeared about the dictionary in the period from September 1961 to May 1962 only.[24]

(c) In 1963 Katz and Fodor published their semantic theory[25] and demanded that dictionaries be organized according to their principles. Their theory influenced the thinking of several leading linguists including Chomsky, and received a great deal of consideration and criticism from others such as Weinteich in "On the semantic structure of language"[26] and Bolinger in "The atomization of meaning."[27] The debate between Katz and Fodor on the one hand and their opponents on the other resulted in new semantic theories such as Weinreich's in "Exploration in semantic theory."[28] Meanwhile new lexicographical methodologies were suggested by eminent linguists such as Charles Fillmore,[29] McCawley,[30] and Hill.[31]

(d) Lexicography has not received attention in linguistic circles only, but in educational institutions as well. In 1966 an English teacher conducted a project entitled, "Lexicographers for a week" in which his eighth-grade students learned the complex skills involved in making a dictionary by compiling a "slang dictionary."[32] Two years later another project is reported which aimed at teaching the eighth graders the purpose of a dictionary, the distinction between prescription and

---

[24] James Sledd and Wilma R. Ebbitt, eds. *Dictionaries and That Dictionary* (Chicago: Scott, Foresman and Co., 1962), p. v.

[25] Jerrold J. Katz and Jerry A. Fodor, "The structure of semantic theory," *Language*, 39 (1963), pp. 170-210.

[26] Uriel Weinreich, "On the semantic structure of language," in *Universals of Language*, ed. by Joseph H. Greenberg (Cambridge, Mass.: M.I.T. Press, 1963), pp. 114-171.

[27] Dwight L. Bolinger, "The atomization of meaning," *Language*, 41 (1965), pp. 555-573.

[28] Uriel Weinreich, "Explorations in semantic theory," in *Current Trends in Linguistics 3*, ed by Thomas A. Sebeok (The Hague: Mouton, 1969), pp. 395-477.

[29] Charles J. Fillmore, "Types of lexical information," in *Working Papers in Linguistics 2*, ed. by Charles J. Fillmore and Ilse Lehiste (Columbus, Ohio: Ohio State Univ., 1968), pp. 65-103.

[30] James D. McCawley, "The role of semantics in a grammar," in *Universals in Linguistic Theory*, ed. by Emmon Bach and Robert T. Harms (New York: Holt, Rinehart and Winston, Inc., 1968), pp. 125-170.

[31] Archibald A. Hill, "Laymen, lexicographers, and linguists," *Language*, 46 (1970), pp. 245-258.

[32] Labota L. Brown, "Junior high lexicographers," *English Journal*, 55 (1966).

description, and the limitation of a dictionary as a recorder rather than
legislator of language change.[33] These two projects are examples of
what is going on in schools all over the nation.

(e) Linguists were not satisfied only with giving courses on lexicography and writing articles and reviews of dictionaries in which they
expressed their views and promoted linguistic principles. They have
sometimes assumed the responsibility of editing dictionaries to set up
a model for the non-linguist lexicographers. An outstanding example
of linguistic editing is Haugen's *Norwegian English Dictionary*[34] which
was compiled in 1965.

(f) Many linguists felt the need for a central lexicographic head-
quarters which assembles all lexicographic materials in a central
computer. In 1967 Lehmann suggested the foundation of a great
dictionary house as an initial step towards producing an updated
dictionary of the scope of *The Century* or the *Oxford English
Dictionary*.[35] In 1968 Sledd called for the formation of the "Lexicography Committee" of the Present-Day English, MLA, which is
exploring the feasibility of Sledd's proposal regarding the foundation
of two lexicographical centers, one in England and the other in the
U.S. to undertake the production of scholarly dictionaries that are
linguistically oriented.[36]

(g) By 1969, it became obvious that lexicography was so attractive
to linguists that the then-president of the Linguistic Society of America,
Hill, dedicated his Presidential Address to it. He said :

> I have tried, in selecting a topic, to steer clear of abstract theory, to find
> a subject where we, as linguists, might reach at least a modicum of
> convergence, and where we might have some hope of affecting, for the
> better, one of the established and institutionalized activities of our culture.
> The area I have chosen is dictionary making...
>
> The most compelling reason for this choice of subject is that, for the
> general public, dictionaries are the most important books that can be
> written about language..."[37]

---

[33] *The Dictionary : Describer of Prescriber? Unit 805* (Minneapolis : Center for
Curriculum Development in English, Minnesota Univ., 1968).

[34] Einar Haugen, ed. *Norwegian English Dictionary* (Madison : Univ. of Wisconsin
Press & Oslo : Universitetsforlaget, 1965).

[35] W. P. Lehman, "Review of two etymological dictionaries," *College English*, 28
(1967), p. 628.

[36] James Sledd, "Dollars and dictionaries," in *New Aspects of Lexicography : Literary
Criticism, Intellectual History, and Social Change*, ed. by Howard D. Weinbort
(Carbondale, Ill. : Southern Illinois University Press, 1971).

[37] Archibald A. Hill, "Laymen, lexicographers, and linguists," *Language*, 46 (1970),
p. 245.

(h) In 1970, the Committee on Lexicography of the Present-Day English Group of the Modern Language Association, and the Linguistic Society of America held a conference on lexicography at Columbus, Ohio, in which a group of linguists discussed serious problems of lexicography and suggested solutions based on scientific research.[38]

(i) On June 5-7, 1972, an International Conference on Lexicography in English was held in New York under the sponsorship of the New York Academy of Sciences, the Modern Language Association, and the Center for Applied Linguistics. The conference was attended by many of the most outstanding linguists of the English-speaking world such as Bolinger, Gleason, Halliday, Haugen, Hill, Joos, Kurath, Lakoff, Lehmann, Malkiel, Marckwardt, McCawley, McDavid, McIntosh, Pike, and Sledd.[39] This is evidence of the fact that lexicography is given serious thought by linguists whose impact on the practice will be felt in the near future.

1.2.2 This book is written to meet a pressing practical need. An urgent reason for selecting the topic stemmed from the observation that most of the linguists' effort is directed toward monolingual lexicography. A survey of linguistic literature related to lexicography shows that, aside from research on machine translation, approximately 90% of it is on monolingual lexicography and the remaining on bilingual lexicography. In 1967, a doctoral dissertation was written under Professor Hill about major linguistic principles (especially semantic) in monolingual lexicography,[40] and it is time to have another study dealing with linguistic treatment of methodological issues in bilingual lexicography, which is "a category raising the greatest variety of disparate problems," as Malkiel said.[41] It is hoped that this book will be of help to those who are engaged in making bilingual dictionaries.

1.3 Scope and Limitations of the Study

With this end in view, numerous bilingual dictionaries of various types and different languages have been studied carefully and their

---

[38] LSA Bulletin, No. 44 (1970), p. 6.

[39] The schedule of the International Conference on Lexicography in English (a mimeograph sent by the Chairman, McDavid to the participants).

[40] Bates Lowry Hoffer III, Linguistic Principles in Lexicography. Unpublished doctoral dissertation, University of Texas at Austin, 1967.

[41] Yakov Malkiel, "Lexicography" in The Learning of Language, ed. by Carroll E. Read (New York: Appleton-Century-Crofts, 1971), p. 369.

technical features examined thoroughly. Major problems that confront bilingual lexicographers have been identified and solutions have been sought in modern linguistic literature. Throughout the book special efforts have been made to provide workable solutions which will result in great improvements. Controversial theories and studies which are still in their infancy have been avoided. Emphasis has been put on valuable theories which are directly related to bilingual lexicography.

Chapter 2 presents a survey of the major typological classifications of dictionaries. Having shown that these classifications are of no help to the lexicographer in his practice (but that they might be of some use in a library cataloguing room) this writer proposes a new linguistically oriented typology of bilingual dictionaries which should be used as a guide to lexicographers in their career. The new typology takes the *purpose* of the bilingual dictionary as a point of departure. The linguistic treatment of the same methodological problem differs from one bilingual dictionary to another depending on the purpose of each one. All the problems raised in the following chapters are dealt with in the light of this typology which can be considered as a unifying theme throughout the book.

Chapter 3 deals with the grammatical problems of the bilingual dictionary. The Chapter is divided into two major sections: the first one is devoted to the problems of phonology, and the other to the problems of morphology and syntax. As is well known, there is a wide range of grammatical problems, therefore the chapter is limited to discussing the following issues: (a) How much phonological information should be provided in a bilingual dictionary and where should it be given? (b) What types of syntactic and morphological information should be available in a bilingual dictionary?

Chapter 4 is devoted to the semantic problems of bilingual dictionaries. Three principal semantic issues are dealt with: (a) The linguistic aspects of translation or, in other words, the characteristics of the ideal translational equivalents. (b) Discrimination of the meaning of polysemous words in the bilingual dictionary. The chapter provides a formula indicating which polysemous word needs meaning discrimination, and suggests precise devices for achieving that discrimination. The devices suggested are both syntactic and semantic. (c) The third semantic problem discussed in this chapter is the question of word family recognition. It is assumed that an attempt should be made in the dictionary to recognize relationships among words in order to facilitate learning and increase retention. Three proposals to achieve this are discussed in this chapter and this writer suggests a new procedure.

Chapter 5 deals with four related issues : usage, illustrative examples, pictorial illustrations, and bilingual lexicography and language teaching. The stand adopted in this book is that a bilingual dictionary should provide information about usage, and make use of illustrative examples and pictorial illustrations. The type of information is indicated and the specifications of contextual examples and pictorial illustrations are determined by the purpose for which the dictionary is being compiled.

CHAPTER TWO

TYPOLOGICAL CLASSIFICATION OF
BILINGUAL DICTIONARIES

2.0   There are many kinds of dictionaries such as glossary, concordance, vocabulary, word book, index, gazetteer, verborum, thesaurus, encyclopaedic dictionary, linguistic atlas, to name a few. Their variety and related terminology have been studied under the rubric of "typology." This chapter presents a survey of the outstanding typological classifications of dictionaries, discusses their usefulness, and proposes a new typology which is more related to bilingual dictionaries and more helpful to the lexicographer and the advancement of bilingual lexicography from the linguistic point of view.

2.1   *Previous Classifications of Dictionaries*

2.1.1   One of the earliest typological studies of dictionaries was made by the Russian linguist L. V. Shcherba in a monograph entitled *Opyt obščej teorii leksikografii*, which was published by the Russian Academy of Sciences in 1940.[1] Shcherba based his classification on the structural characteristics of possible dictionary types. Accordingly he set up a series of six contrasts between these types. The six contrasts are as follows :

(1) A normative dictionary, which dictates norms (such as the dictionaries of the French, Russian, or Spanish Academy) vs. a reference dictionary which adopts a descriptive approach.

(2) An encyclopedia vs. a dictionary. The contrast here is based on the function of proper names in a language. Shcherba thinks that proper names are part of the language and should not be excluded from the dictionary. "The problem is to state their meaning as distinct from the information that an encyclopedia gives about them."[2]

---

[1] L. V. Shcherba, *Opyt obščej teorii leksikografii*. Etjud I. Onsonye tipy slovarej. (= Académie des Sciences de l'URSS, classe de Sciences Littéraires et Linguistiques Bulletin 3 (1940), pp. 89-117.

[2] *Ibid.*, as quoted by Paul L. Garvin in his review of Shcherba's typology, *Word*, 3 (1947), p. 128.

(3) An ordinary dictionary (such as a defining dictionary or translating dictionary) vs. a general concordance in which all the words are listed along with all the quotations that can be found in texts, as is the case in a concordance of a dead language.

(4) A usual dictionary (such as a defining dictionary or a translating dictionary) vs. "ideological" dictionary, which groups ideas or subjects, (such as Roget's Thesaurus).

(5) A defining dictionary (e.g. a monolingual dictionary) vs. a translating dictionary (such as a bilingual or multi-lingual dictionary).

(6) An historical dictionary vs. non-historical dictionary. Shcherba pointed out that the purpose of the historical dictionary is "to give all the meanings of all the words that belong, and have belonged, to a given national language during all of its existence. A dictionary would be an historical one in the true sense of the word if it gave the history of all words during a given period... which would show not only the birth of new words and new meanings, but also their gradual disappearance and their changes. As far as I know," says Shcherba, "no such dictionary exists as yet and the type itself remains to be set up."[3]

Strictly speaking, Shcherba's typology identifies very limited types of dictionaries, seven in number, with broad structural characteristics. This results in a great deal of overlapping among the various types. With the exception of Shcherba's constructive remarks on the historical dictionary and how it should be, his typology presents nothing new, since it is based on the existing dictionaries, and since numerous library catalogues set apart monolingual dictionaries, bilingual dictionaries, concordances, thesauruses, and encyclopedias.

2.1.2 Sebeok made a survey of the dictionaries of the Cheremis language to produce his own typology which makes use of seventeen defining features. Examining this classification with an appraising and expert eye, one can divide these defining features into three subsets of relationships. As Sebeok said :

> The first subset of defining features pertain to the relationship of the lists to the vocabulary intended to be presented. They further pertain to the manner of selection from within the source and to the characteristics of the source itself.[4]

---

[3] *Ibid.*, as quoted by Garvin, p. 129.
[4] Thomas A. Sebeok, "Materials for a typology of dictionaries," *Lingua*, 11 (1962), p. 364.

Accordingly, dictionaries are either (1) *generated*, as when a native lexicographer draws up a selected list of entries which is not based on texts, or (2) *abstracted* from texts. Since an abstracted dictionary tends to transmit the characteristics of its source, these characteristics should be specified and stated in terms of (3) *limits of the corpus*, and (4) *envisaged internal diversity of the corpus*.

The second subset of defining features pertain to the relationship between the components of each entry :

> Within an entry, the object language may be represented by a (5) *single form* or by *multiple forms*. If the object language is represented by multiple forms, the relationship between them may be of two kinds : (6) *based on form*—a dictionary of cognates—...; or (7) based on meaning—a dictionary of synonyms—...[5]

The third subset of defining features pertain to the relationship between entries in the dictionary, i.e., the arrangement of the entries of the book :

> *The sequential arrangement* of the entries can be organized *by* (8) *form* or (9) *meaning*...
>
> *Cross references* provide an alternate arrangement either (10) *according to form*..., or (11) *according to meaning*.[6]

Although the rest of the seventeen defining features do not exhibit relationships, they are either "most closely interrelated with the source features (3) and (4) above,"[7] or they "are less intimately involved in the definition of the dictionary as a type,"[8] as Sebeok himself admits.

One should not lose sight of the fact that Sebeok's study is based on a small number of dictionaries and word lists (twelve only) related to one language only; thus it has several limitations. It is limited in its scope for it mainly deals with few aspects of the lexicographic works, namely the relationship between the dictionary and its sources, the relationship between entries, and the relationship between the language components within each entry. Besides, this classification does not much differ, in its essence, from Malkiel's typology which was taken as "a point of departure" by Sebeok.

2.1.3 The most extensive and most influential typology is Malkiel's classification of dictionaries exemplified by Spanish. It was first

---

[5] *Ibid.*, p. 365.
[6] *Ibid.*, p. 366.
[7] *Ibid.*
[8] *Ibid.*, p. 367.

published in 1959,[9] and later was condensed, modified, and presented at the Indiana Conference on Lexicography under the title "A Typological Classification of Dictionaries on the Basis of Distinctive Features."[10] Malkiel tried to apply procedures which proved useful in classifying phonemes to the typology of lexicographical works. In his own words :

> The obvious model that I had in mind was the separation of a speech sound into a number of distinctive features, ... Was it legitimate to regard a reference book as a bundle of characteristic features which could be reassembled in some kind of arrangement that might be expressed in a simple formula?[11]

Malkiel classifies the existing dictionaries using three criteria : (1) Range, (2) Perspective, and (3) Presentation.

(1) Classification by range : In regard to range, dictionaries are divided by : (a) *density of entries*; which may be measured by the breadth of coverage (how much of the total lexicon of the language is covered?) and by the depth of coverage (how many meanings are listed under each entry? And are contextual connotations and idioms covered?). (b) *number of languages involved*: accordingly, there are mono-, bi-, tri-, quadri-, and pluri- or multilingual dictionaries. (c) *extent of concentration on lexical data*: Malkiel distinguishes encyclopedic data by the inclusion of proper names and by a prodigality of comments which are more than a sober definition needs.[12]

(2) Classification by perspective : Dictionaries can be classified according to (a) *the fundamental dimension*; the dictionary is either synchronic (which is "least contaminated by acknowledged or, worse, unacknowledged archaism") or diachronic (in which the materials are so ordered as to bring out "practically the dynamics of lexical development, with heightened attention to the succession and mutual compatibility of meanings.").

(b) *three contrasting patterns of arrangement*; alphabetic, semantic, or casual (i.e. non-systematic). A combination of the first two is possible, and each pattern may have several subdivisions.

---

[9] Yakov Malkiel, "A typological approach to dictionaries exemplified with Spanish," *Romance Philology*, xii (1959), pp. 366-399; xiii, pp. 111-115.

[10] Yakov Malkiel, "A typological classification of dictionaries on the basis of distinctive features," in *Problems in Lexicography*, ed. by Fred W. Householder and Sol Saporta (Bloomington : Indiana Univ., 1967), p. 3-24.

[11] *Ibid.*, p. 2.

[12] *Ibid.*, pp. 7-15.

(c) *three contrasting levels of tone*; the tone of a dictionary may be detached (reporting facts objectively), preceptive (normative and didactic), or facetious.[13]

(3) Classification by representation : Here dictionaries are classified in the light of their (a) definitions, (b) exemplifications, (c) graphic illustrations (including maps), and (d) special features (localization in territorial terms, on the social scale, or along the axis of "affectivity;" marking of pronunciation).[14]

A serious objection to Malkiel's typology is that it does not result in discrete, mutually opposed dictionary types. Almost all features can co-occur freely in all dictionaries; and thus the analogy between the distinctive features of his typology and the distinctive phonemic features is lost.[15] In actual practice, the distinction between, say, synchronic and diachronic dictionaries is one of degree; most dictionaries contain both descriptive and historical data in varying proportions. Information about these proportions is needed for each dictionary to decide for what purposes it is most useful. This might be one reason why Malkiel was not able to produce the simple formulas he had hoped for.

Another objection to Malkiel's typology pertains to its terminal objectives. Since Malkiel's classification is based on his survey of the existing dictionaries and not on the linguistic requirements for the ideal dictionary, one wonders, with Worth, "whether such a typology might not prove more valuable in the library cataloguing room than in the office of the lexicographer."[16] As a matter of fact, Malkiel himself was aware of this shortcoming when he said, "Ideally, a formal bibliography or a research-library catalogue may well be based on this (or any improved) set of classificatory principles."[17]

Still, one wonders whether bibliographers need such a very extensive classification as Malkiel's.

2.1.4   The French linguist Alain Rey published his general classification of dictionaries in 1970 under the title, "Typologie génétique des dictionnaires." Rey's typology is based on an extensive survey of lexicographical works, but it presents nothing new (in methodology

---

[13] *Ibid.*, pp. 15-20.
[14] *Ibid.*, pp. 20-22.
[15] Dean Stoddard Worth, "Comments," in Householder and Saporta, p. 79.
[16] *Ibid.*
[17] Yakov Malkiel, "A typological classification of dictionaries on the basis of distinctive features," in Householder and Saporta, p. 2.

or content) that has not been dealt with in the typologies of Shcherba, Malkiel, and Sebeok.[18]

2.1.5   Other linguists tend to classify dictionaries on the basis of the amount and type of information contained in the dictionary. Cornyn of Yale University distinguishes only three kinds of dictionary. They are :

> encyclopedic (treating of all aspects of cultural contexts); usage (attempting to portray the morphological and syntactic features); and glossary (a list of forms with a minimum information).[19]

This position seems extreme; it fails to take into account that most of the existing dictionaries are not limited to one type of information, but rather a mixture of two or all of the types mentioned.

Gelb proposes a classification of dictionaries based on the point of view of dictionary makers :

> Thus, we can distinguish the 'philological' dictionaries made by philologists, the 'linguistic' dictionaries made by linguists-anthropologists (social scientists), and the 'general purpose' dictionaries produced by commercial undertakings.[20]

Aside from the difficulty in determining who are meant by the terms "philologist," "linguist," and "social scientist," one can easily find dictionaries made by linguists or philologists but produced by commercial enterprises. Moreover, the proposal does not point out differences among the three suggested types of dictionary themselves.

Mention should also be made of Kiparsky's specialized typology which is restricted to etymological dictionaries.[21]

2.2   A New Typology

2.2.1   In the discussion which follows, this writer will propose a new typology of dictionaries, presenting differences in (a) source, (b) scope, and (c) purpose.

(a) While the previous typologies are based on surveys of the existing dictionaries, the new one is entirely based on the linguists'

---

[18] Alain Rey, "Typologie génétique des dictionnaires," *Langage, 19 : La Lexicographie* (Sept. 1970), pp. 48-68.

[19] William S. Cornyn, "Comments," in Householder and Saporta, p. 274.

[20] I. J. Gelb, "Lexicography, lexicology, and the Accadian dictionary," in *Miscelánea; Homenaje a André Martinet « Estructuralismo E Historia »*, p. 4.

[21] V. Kiparsky, Über etymologische Wörterbücher," *Neuphilologische Mitteilungen, 60* (1959), pp. 209-230; as pointed out by Thomas A. Sebeok, "Materials for a typology of dictionaries," p. 363.

views on lexicography and their criticisms of the existing dictionaries, i.e., how a dictionary should be.

(b) As already stated, all the major typologies deal with all dictionaries. The new proposal is limited to the bilingual dictionary only, in order to serve the ends of this book.

(c) The previous typologies have minimum usefulness or productivity : they do not help the linguist broaden his comprehension of the practical difficulties that confront the lexicographer in his efforts to edit a dictionary, nor do they help the lexicographer understand theoretical solutions offered by linguists, nor do they help the dictionary user select the dictionary that meets his particular needs. The only merit which is claimed for the most extensive typology, i.e. Malkiel's, is that it is an aid to the librarian. The new typology is primarily intended to assist the lexicographer in digesting linguistic theories to produce better bilingual dictionaries. It is also meant to be a guide to the dictionary user in selecting the dictionary which helps him the most.

Strictly speaking, the new typology is based on the purpose or purposes the lexicographer intends to fulfil. A quick survey of linguistic literature related to lexicography in the past ten years shows that linguists recommend different types of bilingual dictionaries and suggest different solutions to the same problem depending on the purpose(s) of the dictionary. Most of the linguists who met at the Indiana Conference on Lexicography made this point directly and clearly. The following is a representative sample of what they said about the issue in question. Martin said :

> You want to make a dictionary that will be concise but exhaustive; exact while not exacting; linguistically adequate for *both* languages, yet uncluttered with trivial details. Sooner or later you have to concentrate on certain goals and forget others. Each dictionary represents some unique compromise, useful—we hope—for some purposes and frustrating for others.[22]

Haas added :

> What is even more deplorable, however, is the fact that often the compilers are not aware of the problems involved. Thinking that they are preparing a dictionary for speakers of both languages, they may easily end up producing a dictionary which is not as useful as it should be to speakers of either language.[23]

---

[22] Samuel E. Martin, "Selection and representation of ready equivalents in a translation dictionary," in Householder and Saporta, p. 153.

[23] Mary R. Haas, "What belongs in a bilingual dictionary?" in Householder and Saporta, p. 47.

To determine the purpose of the dictionary in advance becomes more important when linguists or lexicographers deal with highly specialized problems of bilingual dictionaries. An outstanding example is what Iannucci said about the problem of "meaning discrimination" at the same conference :

> The best way to handle meaning discrimination in any given dictionary should be determined by the kind of use each side of the dictionary is intended.... Various arrangements are possible, the determining factors being for whom the dictionary is intended and for what use or uses it is intended.[24]

Even from the commercial point of view, the publisher of the dictionary determines the customers for whom he intends his book, and designs his dictionary in such a way as to meet their needs. In the words of Barnhart, an experienced commercial lexicographer :

> It is the function of the popular dictionary to answer the questions that the user of the dictionary asks, and the dictionaries on the commercial market will be successful in proportion to the extent to which they answer these questions of the buyer. This is the basis on which the editor must determine the type of information to include.[25]

In fact, the position of the conferees on this point was stated precisely in the opening paragraph of Householder's summary report :

> 1. There were several points on which the conferees expressed unanimity or very general agreement.
> (1) Dictionaries should be designed with a special set of users in mind and for their specific needs. E.g., an English Arabic dictionary for American users for help in speaking Arabic, or a Thai-English dictionary for British and American users for help in reading Thai, etc.[26]

It seems that linguists still hold the same position regarding this issue, and the past twelve years have not brought any fundamental change. Read asserted recently that "a good editor [of a dictionary] must shape his work towards particular goals, depending upon the set of users that he has in mind."[27]

It is obvious from the quotations cited above that linguists distinguish various types of possible or ideal dictionaries depending upon the

---

[24] James E. Iannucci, "Meaning discrimination in bilingual dictionaries," in Householder and Saporta, p. 204.

[25] C. L. Barnhart, "Problems in editing commercial monolingual dictionaries,' in Householder and Saporta, p. 161.

[26] Fred W. Householder, "Summary report," in Householder and Saporta, p. 279.

[27] Allen Walker Read, "Approaches to lexicography and semantics," in *Current Trends in Linguistics*, ed. Thomas A. Sebeok, Volume 10, *Linguistics in North America* (The Hague : Mouton, 1972).

intention of the lexicographer. With this end in view the typology proposed in this book is oriented toward *purpose*.

2.2.2 The classification of bilingual dictionaries proposed here sets up seven contrasts, namely :

(1) Dictionaries for the speakers of the source language vs. dictionaries for the speakers of the target language.

(2) Dictionaries of the literary language vs. dictionaries of the spoken language.

(3) Dictionaries for production vs. dictionaries for comprehension.

(4) Dictionaries for the human user vs. dictionaries for machine translation.

(5) Historical dictionaries vs. descriptive dictionaries.

(6) Lexical dictionaries vs. encyclopedic dictionaries.

(7) General dictionaries vs. special dictionaries.

It should be noted in this connection that the first four contrasts are more related to bilingual dictionaries while the last three are related to both monolingual and bilingual dictionaries. Also, a bilingual dictionary can combine a number of the defining features of these contrasts in accordance with the purposes it is intended to serve. For example, an English-Arabic dictionary can be designed as a tool to help the English-speaking user in speaking Iraqi Arabic with a good coverage of the Iraqi culture. In this case the lexicographer's guiding chart would look as follows :

Dictionary Purposes			
×	Speakers of Source Lg.	Speakers of Target Lg.	
	Literary Lg.	Spoken Lg.	×
×	Production	Comprehension	
×	Human user	Machine trans.	
	Historical	Descriptive	×
×	General	Special	
	Lexical	Encyclopedic	×

As we shall see, the distinction between these types is very necessary for the linguistic treatment of the lexicographical problems discussed in this book. Before proceeding to the analysis of these problems in the light of this typology, a brief account of the important differences between each contrastive pair is given below.

(1) *Dictionaries for the speakers of the source language vs. dictionaries for the speakers of the target language.*

By the source language is meant the language of the entries (the object-language in Sebeok's terminology and the target language in Malkiel's), and the target one is the language of the translations or equivalents (the translating language in Sebeok's terminology and the tool language in Malkiel's). In an English-Arabic dictionary, English is the source language and Arabic is the target one.

The vast majority of the existing bilingual dictionaries, old and new, examined by the writer claim that they are designed to serve the speakers of both languages. The compiler of one of the oldest Arabic-English dictionaries states in his introduction :

> In preparing the first part of this work, my intention has been to compile a compact Arabic dictionary, not only adapted to the wants of English travellers and young students, but also for the use of my own countrymen, who have hitherto had nothing of the kind.[28]

Larousse French and English Modern Dictionary which appeared more than a century later repeated the same thing :

> In its practical format, clarity, and scope, this unique dictionary is indispensable to every French or English speaking person who requires a full command of both languages for business, study, or pleasure.[29]

However, linguists flatly declare that it is impossible to serve the speakers of both languages equally in one and the same bilingual dictionary. As Harrell said :

> A primary problem in the composition of a bilingual dictionary is to decide whether the work is intended for the speakers of X-language or the speakers of Y-language. It is clearly impossible to pay equal attention to both X-speakers and Y-speakers in one and the same work.[30]

One reason why a lexicographer should decide from the very beginning whether X-speakers or Y-speakers are going to use his dictionary is that a bilingual dictionary for the speakers of the source language should be put together in a different way from a bilingual dictionary for the speakers of the target language. In the words of Martin :

> Now it is too much to expect such a dictionary [one that will produce an adequate translation] to work both ways at once. A dictionary that turns

---

[28] Joseph Catafago, *English and Arabic Dictionary* (London : 1858), p. v.

[29] Marguerite-Marie Dubois, (ed.) *Larousse French-English, English-French Modern Dictionary* (Paris : Librairie Larousse, ed. 1969), the front inside cover.

[30] Richard S. Harrell, "Some notes on bilingual lexicography," in Householder and Saporta, p. 51.

out intelligible English (or near-English) sentences for an American who looks up the words in a Japanese sentence will be put together in a different way from one that does the opposite. We must make an early decision: WHO will use the dictionary?[31]

To demonstrate the difference between a dictionary for the speakers of the source language and one for the speakers of the target language, two problems will be cited whose treatment depends upon the type of dictionary. The first issue is "vocabulary selection" (what items are to be entered in the dictionary). Because of the usual limitation on the size of the dictionary, the editor should select his entries in accordance with the purpose of the dictionary. If an English-Arabic dictionary is intended for Americans, there is no point in including the sporting terms of American football, which is unknown in the Arab world. But if the dictionary is designed for the Arabs, these terms may be included in the dictionary since an Arabic learner might encounter some of these terms in their sporting senses in American newspapers and magazines. Another example is provided by Harrell. In the same dictionary cited above such a low frequency English word as *circumnavigate* will not be included in the dictionary if it is primarily intended for the English speaker who wants to learn how to express its meaning in Arabic, because he already knows what it means and can look it up at *sail around* or *go around*.[32] Even if it is included, the English speaker could be referred to *sail around*. But if the dictionary is primarily intended for the Arabic speaker, words like *circumnavigate* should be included in the dictionary to help the user when he encounters these words in his readings.

Another issue which should be treated in two different ways depending upon the type of dictionary is the language of general directions (not only the introduction and the front matter but the directions in individual entries as well). If the dictionary is designed as an aid to the speakers of the source language, then general directions should be given in that language; but if it is meant as an aid to the speakers of the target language, then all the directions should be given in the target language.

Very few dictionaries of limited lexical coverage attempt to serve speakers of both languages with some success. *The German-English,*

---

[31] Samuel E. Martin, "Selection and presentation of ready equivalents in a translation dictionary," in Householder and Saporta, p. 154.

[32] Richard S. Harrell, *op. cit.*, pp. 51-52.

English-German Dictionary of Everyday Usage gives illustrative examples in both languages whenever it is necessary. But this procedure cannot be followed by dictionaries aiming at a broader scope, otherwise the dictionary would become too cumbersome, bulky, and expensive.[33]

(2) *Dictionaries of the literary language vs. dictionaries of the spoken language.*

Modern linguistics has made it clear that speech is the fundamental form of language activity, and writing is just a representation of speech. The argument for this position is neatly stated by Hill:

> Most professional students of language proceed from a few assumptions, one of which is that the fundamental forms of language are the sequences of sounds made by human lips, tongues, and vocal cords—the phenomena usually distinguished by the narrower name of 'speech.' Though this first assumption may seem like a truism, it is important, since many who accept it verbally still act as if they did not believe it. Some few even deny it....
>
> There are a number of facts which should settle this question of priority [between speech and writing]. First, speech reaches back to the origins of human society; writing has only about seven thousand years. Also, no contemporary community of men is without language, even though it is probably still true that most of the world's several thousand language communities remain in the preliterate stage, without benefit of alphabet or even picture symbol. Individual members of literate communities, furthermore, learn their language some years before they learn to read or write it; and adults, even adults who are professional writers, carry on a good deal more speech activity in daily living than activity involving writing.
>
> The final fact is that all writing systems are essentially representations of the forms of speech, rather than representations of ideas or objects in the non-linguistic world.[34]

Examining the existing dictionaries, one can easily conclude that they are based on writing rather than on speech, partly because of the comparative easiness of collecting written materials; thus lexicographers are one example of the people of whom Hill said that they "accept it verbally [but] still act as if they did not believe it." This phenomenon was discussed at the Eighth International Congress of Linguists which

---

[33] *Ibid.*, p. 53.

[34] Archibald A. Hill, *Introduction to Linguistic Structures.* (New York: Harcourt, Brace and Company, 1958), pp. 1-2. It should be pointed out that Professor Hill has recently adopted a different position according to which he considers the 'internal language' as the fundamental form of language. See his article, "Towards a parsing procedure for simple sentences in English," in *Studies in General and Oriented Linguistics*, ed. by Roman Jakobson and Shigeo Kawamoto (Tokyo: TEC Co., 1970), 235-245.

was held in Oslo, August 5-9, 1957. Fries' report at that Conference states :

> In spite of the modern insistence that the materials of speech constitute the 'language,' most practical dictionaries have selected their materials from writing and literature. Only a few of the vocabulary entries carry the label 'colloquial;' and those so marked are often regarded as of a lower level. Frequent discussions have led to a questioning of this approach. Should the basic content vocabulary be that of the language of speech and so assumed without special labels, and the comparatively few items that do not usually occur orally be marked 'literary' or 'bookish?'[35]

One may argue that it is feasible to accommodate the literary and spoken forms of the language in one and the same dictionary by using usage labels. But this is by no means the case. In many speech communities, diglossia exists. Ferguson, who studied this phenomenon in four languages, defines it as :

> A relatively stable situation in which, in addition to the primary dialects of the language (which may include a standard or regional standards), there is a very divergent, highly codified (often grammatically more complex) superimposed variety, the vehicle of a large and respected body of written literature, either of an early period or in another speech community, which is learned largely by formal education and is used for most written and formal spoken purposes but is not used by any sector of the community for ordinary conversation.[38]

In such a situation, where the literary and the spoken languages differ functionally and structurally, it is necessary to deal with them in two separate dictionaries. Moreover the spoken language itself may have a wide range of dialects which differ in their sounds, grammars and vocabulary, as is the case in Arabic;[37] Consequently each dialect should be treated in an independent dictionary.

(3) *Dictionaries for production and dictionaries for comprehension.*

> Despite bulk and good intentions, existing dictionaries lack sufficient information, apparently, to keep a professor of English in Seoul University from writing 'these two vocabularies' when he means 'these two vocabulary items' (or, actually, 'the two words'), or to discourage him from saying 'I have to mail one letter' when he means 'I have a letter to mail.'[38]

---

[35] Charles C. Fries, "Preparation of teaching materials, practical grammars, and dictionaries, especially for foreign languages," in *Proceedings of the Eighth International Congress of Linguists*, ed. by Eva Sivertsen (Oslo : 1958), p. 742.

[36] Charles A. Ferguson, "Diglossia," *Word*, 15 (1959), p. 336.

[37] Peter F. Abboud, "Spoken Arabic," in *Current Trends in Linguistics Vol. 6 : Linguistics in South West Asia and North Africa*, ed. by Thomas A. Sebeok (The Hague : Mouton, 1971), p. 439.

[38] Samuel E. Martin, "Selection and presentation of ready equivalents in a translation dictionary," in Householder and Saporta, p. 154.

Professor Martin's remark can be easily understood if we recall the fact that the traditional approach to foreign language education used to emphasize reading for comprehension rather than speaking or writing for communication. Only a few decades ago, international cooperation was small—people did not feel the need to express themselves in foreign languages. The only exposure to foreign languages was the study of the classics; therefore the dictionary makers assumed that the function of the dictionary was to help the reader in understanding the hard words he came across in his reading of foreign literature. After the turn of the century, technological and other developments in the fields of means of communication, mass media, international relations, and instructional technology gave rise to a new approach to foreign language education which emphasizes expression and communication.[39] Linguists provided the theoretical foundation for the new approach and devised the required methods and techniques such as the direct method, the oral method, and the various audio-lingual methods. Now it is the lexicographers' turn to implement the principles of the new approach in their bilingual dictionaries. It is time for them to make dictionaries which help the user in the production as well as the comprehension of foreign speech and writing.

The distinction between a dictionary for production and one for comprehension is exhibited in the very first stages of making the dictionary; i.e., the choice of source and target languages. Suppose that we are making an English and Arabic dictionary for Americans. If we intend this dictionary as one for production, then English should be our source language and Arabic our target one; whereas if it is meant as a tool for comprehension, Arabic should become the source language and English the target one.

Another difference between the two dictionaries lies in the content and the structure of entries. Asked to make two dictionaries of the same size, one for comprehension and one for production, the lexicographer should include more entries with more senses in the former than in the latter. The entry words in a dictionary for production should be of general productive nature, and their articles should provide the user with more information (than those of a dictionary for comprehension) about the morphological and syntactic behavior of those words. With such a dictionary in hand, the user would not produce

---

[39] Ali M. Al-Kasimi, *Mukhtabaru'l-Lughah* (Kuwait: Daru'l-Qalam, 1970), p. 5.

incorrect sentences like those made by the Korean professor to whom Martin refers.

A dictionary which is intended to help, say, speakers of Persian in both comprehension and production of English sentences should be bidirectional (having two parts : English-Persian and Persian-English). As pointed out in (2), this dictionary would be useful only for speakers of Persian; for speakers of English there should be a different bidirectional dictionary (Persian-English and English-Persian). And thus we may have four different purposes, or simply in the words of Gedney, who summarized the situation in his comment in the third session of the Indiana Conference on Lexicography :

> ...it seems to me there are four main aims open to a bilingual dictionary :
> 1. to tell a speaker of English the meaning of an expression that he hears or reads in the other language;
> 2. to tell a speaker of English how to say something English in the other language;
> 3. to tell a speaker of the other language the meaning of an expression that he hears or reads in English;
> 4. to tell a speaker of the other language how to say something from that language in English.[40]

For practical considerations, dictionaries of dead languages are normally unidirectional (for comprehension) since no Persian, in our example, would need to translate his mother tongue into Old English or any other dead language unless this is meant as a collegiate exercise, which is rare.[41] On the other hand bilingual dictionaries designed for machine translation should be always dictionaries for production.

(4) *Dictionaries for the human user vs. dictionaries for machine translation.*

The development of machine translation highlights several important problems in the bilingual dictionary construction. Computerized dictionaries are a by-product of the effort of linguists in machine translation. There are many essential differences between a dictionary intended for the human user and one intended for machine translation. First, while the former is expected to provide only the necessary information which the dictionary user needs (depending upon the

---

[40] William Gedney, "Comments," in Householder and Saporta, p. 230.

[41] In one of his lectures on lexicography at the University of Texas, Fall 1971, Professor James Sledd remarked that from a theoretical point of view a bidirectional dictionary of a dead language is valuable in comparative historical and cultural studies.

purpose as indicated in (1-4), and this information is usually about the language which is foreign to the user, the dictionary designed for machine translation must contain much more detailed grammatical information about *both* languages.[42] Secondly, the bilingual dictionary which is intended for the human user is permitted to include all or part of the grammatical information in the article, for example, the grammatical behavior of the entry word may be indicated by the use of illustrative examples, but the bilingual dictionary designed for machine translation must incorporate *all* grammatical information in the entry itself, so that the dictionary can function as a kind of sentence generator.[43] Third, while synonymous equivalents might be preferred or allowed in the dictionary intended for the human user for the purpose of stylistic variations, they are strictly avoided in the dictionary designed for machine translation.[44] Fourth, explanations and definitions are allowed and even required in certain cases in the dictionary intended for the human user, but they cannot be included in the dictionary, designed for machine translation, because they lead to complications. Zgusta furnishes a typical example : German *ab holzen* means "clear a wood of trees." If this explanation is included in the memory of the computer, then the translation of the German sentence, "Der wald wurde abgeholzt," will be "The wood was cleared a wood of trees." Instead of that explanation the dictionary should give a translational equivalent, either *deforest*, or *disforest*.[45]

With this distinction in view, this book is dealing with dictionaries for the human user, though many linguistic principles discussed are applicable to both types.

(5) *Historical dictionaries vs. descriptive dictionaries.*

The purpose of any dictionary is to describe objectively the lexicon of a language either in its present state (here such a dictionary is given the label "descriptive") or as it was in one or more of its previous periods (such a dictionary is here called "historical"). The historical dictionary has been given various names such as "prescriptive," "normative," "didactic" and the like. Leaving terminology aside, the defining characteristics of the historical dictionary are :

---

[42] Samuel E. Martin, "Selection and presentation of ready equivalents in a translation dictionary," in Householder and Saporta, p. 154.

[43] *Ibid.*, p. 153.

[44] Ladislav Zgusta, "Idle thoughts of an idle fellow or diversions of MT lexicography," Austin : Linguistic Research Center, University of Texas, 1971, pp. 5-6.

[45] *Ibid.*

(a) The sources of the dictionary are written materials or records that belong to a past period of the language, and the information it presents on pronunciation is based on those records. As a result the dictionary will include obsolete expressions.

(b) When the dictionary provides etymologies, it leaves description and goes to history.

(c) The quotations cited in the historical dictionary are limited to a certain previous period or periods of the language.

(d) The historical dictionary arranges the senses of its entries in such a way as to show how meanings have developed from one another. In other words the semantics of the dictionary is historically oriented. On the other hand, a purely descriptive dictionary derives its materials, pronunciations, and quotations from its own age; arranges its senses according to frequency or any other descriptive criterion; and does not deal with etymology.[46]

The first great European dictionaries were historical in their approach. The historical approach was originated in Italy by *Vocabolario degli accademici della crusca* (1591-1612), and developed in France and England by the *Dictionnaire de l'Académie Française* (1694) and Samuel Johnson's *Dictionary of English Language* (1755).[47] Nowadays, most dictionaries combine historical and descriptive features. Pure historical dictionaries can be exemplified by period dictionaries. In 1919 Dr. W. A. (later Sir William) Craigie came up with the notion of period dictionaries for the first time. He stated that the *Oxford English Dictionary* in its attempt to cover the whole history of English could not do justice to any one period. So he proposed that there should be a series of dictionaries of different historic periods such as Old English dictionary, Middle English dictionary, Early Modern English Dictionary, and the like. As he said before the Philological Society in London :

> Yet each definite period of the language has its own characteristics, which can only be appreciated when it is studied by itself, and which are necessarily obscured when it merely comes in as one link in the long chain of the language as a whole. To deal adequately with each period it is necessary to take it by itself and compile for it a special dictionary, as full and complete as may be.[48]

---

[46] Professor James Sledd's lectures on Lexicography at the University of Texas, Fall 1971, taped by the writer.

[47] *Ibid.*

[48] *Transactions of the Philological Society* (1925-30), pp. 6-9.

Although the available period dictionaries are monolingual such as the *Middle English Dictionary*,[49] bilingual period dictionaries are practically feasible and theoretically defensible. Generally speaking, bilingual dictionaries for production should be descriptively oriented, whereas those for comprehension can be of both types, historical or descriptive.

(6) *Lexical dictionaries vs. encyclopedic dictionaries.*

In terms of their inclusion of encyclopedic information, dictionaries can be categorized into : (a) lexical dictionaries, and (b) encyclopedic dictionaries. The first time the adjective "encyclopedic" appeared in the English language was in Robert Hunter's *Encyclopedic Dictionary* which was begun in 1872 and completed in 1889.[50] *The Century Dictionary*, which was the first encyclopedic dictionary in the U.S., and the third of its kind in the English-speaking world, cites three defining characteristics of encyclopedic information :

(a) inclusion of names of persons, places, and literary works;

(b) coverage of all branches of knowledge; and

(c) extensive treatment of facts.[51]

Both encyclopedic dictionaries and encyclopedias include encyclopedic information. But while in encyclopedias the information is presented under a few general topics, in encyclopedic dictionaries it is distributed under a large number of headings to which it is related.[52] It is claimed that the distribution of the encyclopedic material under the individual words and phrases makes each item of the encyclopedic information more accessible than in encyclopedias.[53] Another difference between them is that the encyclopedic dictionary presents the information "more concisely than a full-scale encyclopedia does."[54]

When the term "encyclopedic dictionary" is mentioned, one thinks of unabridged dictionaries such as *The Century Dictionary* and the *Oxford English Dictionary*. As for the abridged dictionaries, the encyclopedic information is measured by the inclusion of proper

---

[49] Hans Kurath, ed., *Middle English Dictionary* (Ann Arbor : Univ. of Michigan Press, 1952-).

[50] Philip B. Gove, "The nonlexical and the encyclopedic," *Names*, 13 (1965), p. 106.

[51] William D. Whitney, ed., *The Century Dictionary*, the articles on "encyclopedia" and "encyclopedic."

[52] *ibid.*, p. iv.

[53] *Ibid.* Publisher's note on the completed work.

[54] James R. Hulbert, *Dictionaries : British and American* (Tonbridge, Kent : Andre Deutsch Ltd., 1955), p. 33.

nouns and culture items because there is not enough space for extensive treatment of facts. The distinction between proper nouns and common nouns no longer presents a difficulty. Although Jespersen remarked that "linguistically it is utterly impossible to draw a sharp line of demarcation between proper names and common names,"[55] generally speaking, semantically, a common noun can be defined as a name of a class whereas a proper noun is the name of an individual; and formally and syntactically they can be distinguished by the presence of a determiner or article before common nouns, and their absence before proper nouns,[56] (there are exceptions; see Hill's "re-examination of the English articles).[57]

Several scholars object to the inclusion of encyclopedic materials in the dictionary. A professional lexicographer, Gove, said :

> A one-volume dictionary and encyclopedia combined is not feasible and not even sustainable without facilities now unavailable and a type of research not now being carried on.[58]

As far as bilingual dictionaries are concerned, this writer thinks that they should include proper nouns and other cultural items for the following reasons :

(a) It might be easy for the reader of a foreign language to tell whether a lexical unit is a proper noun or not if capitalization of proper names is used in that language; but is is not so easy when the foreign language he is reading does not use capitalization as is the case in Arabic. The reader will look up the hard word (a proper noun or otherwise) in his bilingual dictionary. On the spoken level, names of persons and places do not always have similar pronunciation in different languages.

(b) Experience has shown that encyclopedic information related to the foreign language is more often looked for in the bilingual dictionary, and if Gove's principle which states that "the function of a dictionary is to serve the person who consults it,"[59] is accepted, encyclopedic information should be provided in the bilingual dictionary. Linguists

---

[55] Otto Jespersen, *Philosophy of Grammar* (London : G. Allen & Unwin, Ltd., 1924), p. 69.

[56] Leonard Bloomfield, *Language* (New York : Holt, Rinehart and Winston, 1933), p. 205.

[57] Archibald A. Hill, "A re-examination of the English articles," *Monograph Series on Language and Languages*, 19 (1966), pp. 217-231.

[58] Philip B. Gove, "The nonlexical and the encyclopedic," *Names*, 13 (1965), p. 108.

[59] Philip B. Gove, "The dictionary's function," in *The Role of the Dictionary*, ed. by Philip B. Gove (Indianapolis : The Bobbs-Merrill Co., Inc., 1967), p. 5.

who edited bilingual dictionaries were aware of the fact that the inclusion of encyclopedic materials contributes to the general usefulness of the dictionary. One of the best bilingual dictionaries edited by linguists in the U.S. recently is Haugen's *Norwegian-English Dictionary* which includes "common abbreviations, ...important place and proper names, ...and cultural features."[60]

Yorkey emphasizes the practical necessity of the inclusion of encyclopedic materials in a dictionary intended for foreign students. He says:

> He [the foreign student] needs information about the famous persons and places, both real and literary, that native speakers respond to as part of their cultural heritage and education.... If he comes across a reference to Old Glory, Bucephalus, Mrs. Malaprop, Madison Avenue, or every Tom, Dick and Harry, he cannot be expected to rush to the library and look it up [in encyclopedias, gazetteers, and almanacs]. He needs the reference immediately. He needs the reference in a dictionary right here on his desk.[61]

(7) *General dictionaries vs. special dictionaries.*

A general dictionary is one which attempts the coverage of the whole lexicon of the language whereas a special dictionary deals with one sector of the lexicon. In a general dictionary, the vocabulary of all fields of knowledge should be represented and the reading of the public to which the dictionary is intended should be also sampled. On the other hand the purpose of the special dictionary is to help the user to acquaint himself with the meaning of the jargon and the terminology of a special field; e.g. Hitti's *English-Arabic Dictionary of Medical Terminology*[62] or Shihabi's *Dictionary of Agricultural Terms.*[63] Special bilingual dictionaries are very useful in the developing countries where scientific and technical terminology is translated from other languages. Such dictionaries are essential for both professional translators and laymen.

---

[60] Einar Haugen, ed. *Norwegian-English Dictionary* (Madison: University of Wiscons, in Press, 1965), p. 9.

[61] Richard Yorkey, "Which desk dictionary is best for foreign students of English?" *TESOL Quarterly*, 3 (1969), p. 258.

[62] Joseph D. Hitti, *English-Arabic Dictionary of Medical Terminology* (Beirut, 1967).

[63] Mustafa al-Shihabi, *Dictionary of Agricultural Terms* (Damascus, 1957).

CHAPTER THREE

GRAMMATICAL PROBLEMS
IN THE BILINGUAL DICTIONARY

3.0   A commonplace statement in linguistics is that grammar (sound structure included) and lexicon are the two major portions of language structure.[1] The relation of lexicon and grammar varies considerably from one linguistic theory to another. Chomsky's grammar, for example, would include a lexicon within itself. Chomsky stated that a grammar "contains a base consisting of a categorial component and a lexicon. The lexicon consists of lexical entries, each of which is a system of specified features."[2] In Bloomfield's terminology, grammar and lexicon are two important parts of linguistic description and that the "lexicon is really an appendix of the grammar, a list of basic irregularities."[3]

Although a strict separation of lexicon and grammar is seldom "in the best long-term interest of smooth language learning,"[4] it is desirable for certain operations to draw a basic theoretical distinction between them.[5] In this connection, there are three misleading statements about the difference between a grammar and a dictionary :

(a) A dictionary is concerned with words only and a grammar with everything else. This statement might have been caused by a misunderstanding of such definitions of grammar as Fries's :

> The total linguistic meaning of any utterance consists of the lexical meanings of the separate words plus such structural meanings.... *The grammar of a language consists of the devices that signal structural meanings.*[6]

---

[1] Yakov Malkiel, "Lexicography," in *The Learning of Language*, ed. by Carroll E. Reed (New York : Appleton-Century-Crofts, 1971), p. 368.

[2] Noam Chomsky, "Remarks on nominalization," in *Readings in English Transformational Grammar*, ed. by Roderick A. Jacobs and Peter S. Rosenbaum (Waltham, Massachusetts : Ginn and Company, 1970), pp. 184-185.

[3] Leonard Bloomfield, *Language* (New York : Holt, 1933), p. 274.

[4] Yakov Malkiel, *op. cit.*, p. 368.

[5] Madeleine Mathiot, "The place of the dictionary in linguistic description," *Language*, 43 (1967), p. 703.

[6] Charles C. Fries, *The Structure of English* (New York : Harcourt, Brace & World, Inc., 1952), p. 56.

The above-cited statement about the difference between a grammar and a dictionary is misleading because in reality both grammar and dictionary deal with words.[7]

(b) A dictionary deals with the lexical items of a language and a grammar with the abstract relations into which these lexical items enter. This statement might have risen from a misunderstanding of some definitions of grammar like Francis's :

> By grammatical structure is meant the organizing of morphemes and words into larger meaningful utterances. Grammar, then, can be defined as the branch of linguistics which deals with the organization of morphemic units into meaningful combinations larger than words.[8]

This second statement about the difference between a grammar and a dictionary is not true either, because both dictionary and grammar are concerned with the lexical items of language and the abstract relations into which they enter.[9]

(c) The third misleading statement which is widespread is that a grammar is concerned with form and a dictionary with meaning. This statement is not accurate because actually there is a great deal of overlapping between a grammar and a dictionary : the grammatical statement includes the meanings of constructional patterns, inflectional affixes, and derivational morphemes; and the dictionary does not list the words of the language along with their meanings only, but gives formal information about their structural behavior as well.[10] Besides, form and meaning are not opposed to each other but instead complement each other.[11]

In the light of Bloomfield's definition of lexicon as "an index to the grammar," the difference between a grammar and a dictionary can be stated in terms of class versus member. The grammar sets up classes (and subclasses) and takes care of all relationships between them. The dictionary will be responsible for matters pertaining to the members of classes such as the identification of the class (and subclasses) to which a lexical item belongs.[12] The contemporary British linguistic

---

[7] Halliday, M. A. K., Angus McIntosh, and Peter Strevens, *The Linguistic Science and Language Teaching* (Bloomington : Indiana University Press, 1965), p. 22.

[8] W. Nelson Francis, *The Structure of American English* (New York : The Ronald Press Company, 1958), p. 223.

[9] Halliday, McIntosh, and Strevens, *op. cit.*

[10] H. A. Gleason, Jr., "The relation of lexicon and grammar," in Householder and Saporta, pp. 90-91.

[11] Halliday, McIntosh, and Strevens, *op. cit.*, p. 23.

[12] H. A. Gleason, Jr., *op. cit.*, p. 94.

school adopts a similar position in this connection. They state the difference between a grammar and a dictionary as follows :

> ...grammar deals with closed system choices, which may be between items ('this/that,' 'I/you/he/she/we/they') or between categories (singular/plural, past/present/future); lexis with open set choices, which are always between items ('chair/settee/bench/stool' etc.).[13]

To the linguists of this British school of thought, closed sets can be easily stated in abstractions and generalizations, whereas open sets do not lend themselves easily to generalizations. Consequently a grammatical statement can cover a greater number of linguistic events than a lexical statement.[14] Taking this statement into consideration, one can see the similarity between their position and that of Bloomfield, who considers the lexicon as "a list of basic irregularities." This doctrine can be taken as a safe guide by lexicographers in dealing with grammatical problems in their dictionaries.

The present chapter is devoted to some major grammatical problems. For convenience it is divided into two major sections : 3.1 Phonology and 3.2 Morphology and Syntax.

3.1   *Phonology*

3.1.1   The vast majority of dictionaries today provide some kind of information about pronunciation, usually a respelling of each entry word. Some consider pronunciation as the basic formal distinction between unabridged encyclopedic dictionaries and encyclopedias : dictionaries provide information about pronunciation because it is an essential part of the linguistic description, whereas encyclopedias are not supposed to indicate the pronunciation of each item.[15] Special dictionaries of pronunciation like Kenyon and Knott[16] are no longer as useful as they once were because general dictionaries have answered that need.

Pronunciation was not one of the functions of the early English dictionaries. Bailey introduced stress for the first time into his *Dictionarium Britannicum* in 1736. He marked the main stress over entry

---

[13] Halliday, McIntosh, and Strevens, *op. cit.*, p. 23.

[14] *Ibid.*

[15] W. Cabell Greet, "Pronunciation," in *The American College Dictionary*, ed. by C. L. Barnhart (New York : Random House, 1967), p. xx.

[16] John S. Kenyon and Thomas A. Knott, *A Pronouncing Dictionary of American English* (Springfield, Mass. : G. & C. Merriam Co., 1944).

words.[17] This technique was borrowed by Johnson in his *Dictionary of the English Language* in which the only phonetic clue given was the primary stress which was indicated "by printing an accent upon the acute or elevated syllable;"[18] and a few directions about the irregularities of certain sounds which were given in the front matter. Pronunciation of words had to wait until 1773 when Kenrick introduced it in his work, *A New Dictionary of the English Language*.[19] He placed diacritical marks and numerals over entry words to indicate pronunciation. Vocalic nuclei, for example, were indicated by numerals referring to key words; two accents, the acute and the grave, were used; and italic type was employed to show the incidence of consonantal phonemes. But Kenrick altogether omitted a large number of words whose pronunciation was doubtful or difficult.[20] Lexicographers went on using several diacritical marks, such as dots, curves, and numbers, which were placed over or under the letters of the entry word to show when a letter was silent, when a vowel was long, etc. This method proved unsatisfactory because of the large number of diacritical marks that were used, and because those marks caused trouble to the writer, printer, proofreader, and dictionary user.[21] Therefore, toward the end of the nineteenth century, lexicographers started to respell the whole word using a phonetic key of symbols.[22]

3.1.2 The need for information about pronunciation in dictionaries has been increased by new attitudes about speech. The printed word is no longer the only means of mass communication; the spoken word has become as important in the age of radio, telephone, phonograph, television, tape recorder, video tape recorder, cinema, and telstar. Rhetoric, which for some time meant the rules of written composition only, is regaining its other meaning, "oratory." In 1955 Barnhart circulated 108 questionnaires in 99 American colleges concerning the types of information commonly provided in monolingual college

---

[17] Stewart A. Steger, *American Dictionaries* (Baltimore : J. H. Furst Co., 1913), p. 13.

[18] Samuel Johnson, *A Dictionary of the English Language* (London : 1833), p. 3.

[19] William Kenrick, *A New Dictionary of the English Language*, (London : William Johnston, Longman, Cadell and the Rivingtons, 1773).

[20] James Sledd and Gwin J. Kolb, *Dr. Johnson's Dictionary : Essays in the Biography of a Book* (Chicago : The Univ. of Chicago Press, 1955), 173-174.

[21] Isaac K. Funk, *New "Standard" Dictionary* (New York : Funk & Wagnalls, 1963), p. xii.

[22] William Allen Neilson, ed. *Webster's New International Dictionary of the English Language*, Second Edition (Springfield, G. & C. Merriam Co., 1934), p. xii.

dictionaries. The results indicated that 56,000 students considered pronunciation third in importance (after meaning and spelling) among the six types of information.[23] If this is the case with native speakers of the language, one can rightly imagine that information about pronunciation is more important for the foreign learner of the language. If he uses his bilingual dictionary to produce the foreign language he certainly wants to know the appropriate word and how to pronounce it. And if he comes across a hard word in his reading, then he wants to know what it means and most probably how to say it as well.

A respelling is necessary to provide adequate information about pronunciation. This is due to the fact that although most spelling systems are phonemic in principle they are faulty and incomplete. In his valuable article, "The typology of writing systems," Hill pointed out two important facts :

(a) Most of the writing systems in the world attempt to record primarily the segmental phonemes; but they overlook the supra-segmental phonemes such as separator, stress, and pitch. Consequently these writing systems are incomplete.

(b) Most of the writing systems no longer "faithfully record all phonemic contrasts in the language in a systematic fashion."[24] Although existing writing systems are basically phonetic (i.e. each character stands for a sound), they allow very many exceptions. For instance, there is no item-to-item correspondence between English sounds and spellings.[25] According to Barnhart, English has 44 sounds represented by 251 spellings. An outstanding example is the phoneme /š/ which is represented by 14 spellings such as : ce (ocean), sch (schist), sci (conscience), se (nauseous), sh (ship), si (mansion), ss (tissue), ssi

---

[23] C. L. Barnhart, "Problems in editing commercial monolingual dictionaries," in Householder and Saporta, p. 161. The other three types of information listed in Barnhart's questionnaires are synonym studies and lists, usage notes, and etymologies.

[24] Archibald A. Hill, "The typology of writing systems," in *Papers in Linguistics in Honor of Léon Dostert*, ed. W. Austin (The Hague : Mouton, 1967) pp. 96-97.

[25] A contrary position is held by Wayne O'Neal who argues that "English orthography is nearly optimal, not at the level of phonetic or actual pronunciation, but at an abstract level, a psychologically significant level from which pronunciation can be predicted and to which they can be referred." ("The spelling and pronunciation of English," in *American Heritage Dictionary*, p. xxxv). However, even if this could be proved, it does not deny the need for pronunciation transcription in the dictionary because the process of deriving English pronunciation from orthography requires the application of "a complicated set of rules" which the dictionary user cannot perform at every opening.

(mission), ti (mention), and chsi (fuchsia).[26] One reason why there is no item-to-item correspondence between sound and spelling is the unbroken length of orthographic tradition of the language. While the sounds of the language undergo constant change and growth, the writing system is rarely reviewed or adapted to recent changes in speech. Consequently, there is a patent need for a transcription in linguistic research and dictionaries.

3.1.3 Linguists agree that the main principles of any transcription are two :

(a) every distinct sound of the language should be represented by a distinct symbol, and

(b) no sound should be represented in more than one way.[27]

In other words, any transcription should have the twofold merit of simplicity and accuracy, in addition to the requirement of completeness.

There are two types of transcription : phonemic (or broad) and phonetic (or narrow). In a phonemic transcription, "the symbols give the sounds which form contrasts in the language, disregarding varieties which do not form contrasts."[28] On the other hand, a phonetic transcription takes care of all or most varieties of sounds. Using a bit of linguistic terminology, a phonemic transcription represents the phonemes of the language whereas a phonetic one records the allophones of the language as well. A phonemic transcription is limited to those distinctive differences or contrasts which are capable of distinguishing one meaning from another in the language such as the initial sound units of /pɪn/ and /bɪn/; whereas a phonetic transcription records also all the nondistinctive differences such as an aspirated [p'] in pin, an unaspirated [p⁼] in spin, and an unreleased [p'] in napkin.[29]

The bilingual lexicographer is confronted from the very beginning with the question "Should a phonemic or phonetic transcription be used in the dictionary? Is not a purely phonetic notation just as good, and more accurate?" Some theoreticians think that since the use of the right allophones distinguishes native from foreign speakers, and since the foreign language learner should aim at approximating native speech,

---

[26] C. L. Barnhart, ed. *The American College Dictionary* (New York : Random House, 1967), p. xxvii.

[27] Archibald A. Hill, *Oral Approach to English*, Vol. 1 (Tokyo: The English Language Education Council, Inc., 1965, 1966), "Principles of Transcription," pp. 5-13.

[28] *Ibid.*, p. 5.

[29] Bernard Bloch and George L. Trager, *Outline of Linguistic Analysis* (Baltimore, Md. : Linguistic Society of America, 1942), p. 38.

the bilingual dictionary should present a phonetic description of the language.[30] Others feel that the linguists' task is to classify the facts of language and to present the foreign learner with the really significant features of speech rather than the accidental and personal. In supporting the position of phonemic rather than phonetic description, Bloch and Trager concluded by saying :

> The reason for preferring a phonemic to a purely phonetic description, then, is wholly practical. By organizing the countless details of pronunciation into a small number of distinctive units, the student not only simplifies the learning process, but actually achieves a better practical command of the language than he could by any other method in the same amount of time. This statement does not rest on theory; it is borne out by the experience of all students who have used the phonemic approach in their study of a foreign language.[31]

There is much truth in both positions, and most linguists today would probably accept some combination of the two approaches to secure both accuracy and simplicity, although a few may align themselves exclusively behind one or another. A sensible approach would be : The front matter of the dictionary should deal with the phonemic and phonetic sides of the phonological description of the language; it should present the phonemes of that language and under each one its chief allophones and their complementary distribution. As for the transcription of the materials in the body of the dictionary, it should be always phonemic except where the foreign learner is expected to go seriously wrong without additional reminder, i.e. phonetic symbols.[32] The identification of those phonological features which need additional phonetic reminders depends upon a contrastive analysis of the sound systems of the source and target languages.

The second phonological problem which the lexicographer encounters is : "Which of the existing phonemic transcriptions fits the bilingual dictionary best?" In linguistic research, one finds several different approaches to phonological description due to different analyses. Taking English phonology as an example, one finds that the most usual transcriptions differ mainly in their symbols for vowels and composites (see Table 2). It is well known that English vowels can differ in their length (the amount of time given to their pronunciation) and in their quality. When the quality of the vowel is considered

---

[30] Kemp Malone, "Structural linguistics and bilingual dictionaries," in Householder and Saporta, p. 115.

[31] Bernard Bloch and George L. Trager, *Outline of Linguistic Analysis*, p. 40.

[32] Kemp Malone, *op. cit.*, pp. 115-117.

	Jones	Scott	Ward, Palmer	Pike	Fries	Kenyon	Thomas	MacCarthy	Trager and Smith	Hill	Bloomfield	Bloch and Trager	Sledd
seat	i:	i:	i	i	i	i	i	ii	iy	iy	ij	ij	i:
sit/silk	i	i	ɪ	ι	ɪ	ɪ	ɪ	i	i	i/ɨ	i	i	ɪ/ɨ
say	ei	ei	eɪ	e	e	e	e	ei	ey	ey	ej	ej	e:
set	ɛ	e	ɛ	ɛ	ɛ	ɛ	ɛ	e	e	e	e	e	ɛ
sat	a	a	æ	æ	æ	æ	æ	a	æ	æ	ɛ	a	æ/æ:
salve	–	–	–	–	–	a	–	–	æh	–	–	–	–
suit/food	u:	u:	u	u	u	u	u	uu	uw	uw	uw	uw	u:
soot/put	u	u	ʊ	ʊ	ʊ	ʊ	ʊ	u	u	u	u	u	ʊ
so	ou	ou	ου	o	o	o	o	ou	ow	ow	ow	ow	o/o:
sought/saw	ɔ:	ɔ:	ɔ	ɔ	ɔ	ɔ	ɔ	oo	ɔh	ɔh	ɔ	oh	ɔ:
sot/not	ɔ	ɔ	ɒ	–	–	ɒ	ɒ	o	ɔ	ɔ	ɑ	o	ɑ/ɔ
psalm/calm	ɑ:	a:	ɑ	a	a	ɑ	ɑ	aa	ah	ah	a·	ah	ɑ:
sun	ʌ	ʌ	ʌ	ə	ə	ʌ	ʌ	ʌ	ə	ə	o	ə	ə/ɑ
the	ə	ə	ə	ə	ə	ə	ə	ə	ə	ə	ə/o	ə	ə/ɨ
sir (RP)	ə:	ə:	ɜ	–	–	ɜ	ɜ	əə	əh	–	–	əh	ə:
sir (*)	–	–	–	r	ər	ʒ	ɜˋ	–	ər	ər	ər	ər	ə:r
lesser (*)	–	–	–	r	ər	əˋ	əˋ	–	ər	ər	r	r	ər
sigh	ɑi	ai	aɪ	aⁱ	aɪ	aɪ	aɪ	ai	ay	ay	aj	aj	ɑi/ai
sow/now	ɑu	au	aυ	aᵘ	aυ	aυ	aυ	au	aw	aw	aw	aw	ɑu/au
soy/boy	ɔɪ	oi	ɔɪ	oⁱ	ɔɪ	ɔɪ	ɔɪ	oi	ɔy	oy	ɔj	oj	ɔi/oi
ship	ʃ	ʃ	ʃ	š	š	ʃ	ʃ	ʃ	š	š	š	š	š
measure	ʒ	ʒ	ʒ	ž	ž	ʒ	ʒ	ʒ	ž	ž	ž	ž	ž
church	tʃ	tʃ	tʃ	č	č	tʃ	tʃ	tʃ	č	č	č	tš/č	č
judge	dʒ	dʒ	dʒ	ǰ	ǰ	dʒ	dʒ	dʒ	ǰ	ǰ	ǰ	dž/ǰ	ǰ
thin	θ	θ	θ	θ	θ	θ	θ	θ	θ	θ	θ	θ	θ
then	ð	ð	ð	ð	ð	ð	ð	ð	ð	ð	ð	ð	ð
young	j	j	j	j	y	j	j	j	y	y	j	j	y
which	hw		ʍ	hw	hw	hw	hw		hw				
huge	hj		hj		hy	hj	ç		hy				

Table 2: Comparison of the Most Usual Styles of English Phonetic Notation
(*) Gen. Amer.

(From Mackey's *Language Teaching Analysis*, p. 54)

distinctive, its length will be redundant. When a transcriber takes length into consideration he tends to show that two symbols for contrastive phonemes differ in length only. For example, according to the IPA notation *pit* and *Pete* are transcribed as follows : /pit/ : /pi:t/ which indicates that the two vowels differ in length, /i/ : /i:/. On the other hand a transcriber who takes quality into account tends to give two different symbols to those contrastive phonemes, as in Kenyon and Knot's notation, /pɪt/ : /pit/. A linguist who wants to show in his transcription (for pedagogical reasons) both length and quality may do as Hill did, /pɪt/ : /piyt/. The two symbols differ in shape and length. As Hill explained :

> ...the /ɪ/ of *pit* differs from the /i/ of *Pete* since the vowel of *Pete* is tenser and higher than the vowel of *pit*. The /i/ of *Pete* is followed by /y/ because the second part of the nucleus of *Pete* is a diphthongal glide to a high front position which is the starting point of the semi-vowel in *yes*. In *Pete* the /y/ is the reverse of the downward glide in *yes*. The transcription of *Pete* uses two symbols, whereas *pit* uses one. The two symbols indicate not only that the nucleus in *Pete* is a diphthong rather than a pure vowel, but that the nucleus in *Pete* is longer, since it contains two sounds rather than one.[33]

This type of notation which attracts the attention of the foreign learner to all of the differences between words avoids making decisions on which difference is distinctive and which is redundant. The difference between the three notations cited above persists throughout all the vowels. The following table exemplifies this difference :

	IPA	*Kenyon & Knot*	*Hill*
pit	/pit/	/pɪt/	/pɪt/
Pete	/pi:t/	/pit/	/piyt/
pet	/pet/	/pɛt/	/pɛt/
Pate	/pe:t/	/pet/	/peyt/
full	/ful/	/fʊl/	/fʊl/
fool	/fu:l/	/ful/	/fuwl/
bought	/bɔ:t/	/bɔt/	/bɔt/
boat	/bout/	/bot/	/bowt/[34]

The other major point where transcriptions differ is the two composite consonants /č/ and /ǰ/. They are called composites because each is made up of two sounds : /č/ is made up of /t/ followed by /š/, and

---

[33] Archibald A. Hill, *Oral Approach to English*, Vol. 1, p. 7.
[34] *Ibid.*, pp. 6-7.

/ǰ/ is made up of /d/ followed by /ž/. A linguist who considers /č/ and /ǰ/ as phonemic units represents them with single symbols, whereas if their unitary quality was denied, they would be transcribed as in IPA where they are represented by /ts/ and /dz/.[35] For pedagogical purposes Hill has recently transcribed /č/ and /ǰ/ as /tš/ and /dž/.

Taking all the differences into account, one can conclude that a bilingual dictionary should employ the Hill transcription for English and a similar transcription which is based on the same principles for other languages, because it reminds the foreign language learner of all the features of the transcribed sounds and consequently facilitates learning.

It is obvious that one notation should be used throughout the dictionary. To use more than one respelling system would lead to confusion. Still one can find dictionaries which use two notations at the same time. An outstanding example is the 1958 edition of Funk and Wagnall's *New "Standard" Dictionary of the English Language* in which each word is respelled twice, the first in the Revised Scientific (or National Education Association) Alphabet, and the second in what is commonly known as the "textbook key." This step was taken because the dictionary was in "a period of transition from the second or old key to the new."[36] It should be also borne in mind that a notation system used in a bilingual dictionary should not be complicated, since the key is not before the user of the dictionary at each opening.[37]

It is customary that a dictionary should include in its front matter a section on how to make use of the notation employed, and should exemplify each symbol by one or more key words. A complicated notation system and badly selected key words can make the phonological information provided in the dictionary quite useless, if not worse. In a notation used by a best-seller English-Arabic dictionary,[38] the letter (a), for instance, is assigned for five various vowels and diphthongs: ă, ā, â, ä, à, and the character (o) appears in eight different sounds: ŏ, ō, ô, oe, oi, ŏo, ōo, ou, and so on. Besides, many of the key words cited in that dictionary fail to function as illustrations. For example:

---

[35] *Ibid.*, p. 6.

[36] Funk and Wagnall's *New "Standard" Dictionary of the English Language*, p. xii.

[37] James Sledd, "The lexicographer's uneasy chair," in *Dictionaries and That Dictionary* ed. by James Sledd and Wilma R. Ebbitt (Chicago: Scott, Foresman, 1962), p. 234.

[38] Munir Ba'albaki, ed., *Al Mawrid: A Modern English-Arabic Dictionary* (Beirut: Dar El-Ilm Lil-Malayēn, 1967).

"â   aware, ...
à   à bas, aperitif"

Which of the two vowels in (aware) is meant to be the key sound of â,
and how can a Saudi or Iraqi learner of English figure out the pronunciation of the French phrase "à bas?"[39] The key words should be
familiar and have the same pronunciations in all major dialects if
possible. The writer of this book suggests that a bilingual dictionary
should include a record or a tape which contains all the key words
and sentences pronounced by a native speaker of the target language.

3.1.4 Linguists agree that a bilingual dictionary should provide
phonological information as a part of language description, but
opinions are split on the amount of that information. An analysis of
their attitudes towards this question shows three distinct positions :

(a) The first recommends the transcription of the whole entry word.
This is the position of existing dictionaries. Such transcription usually
shows syllabification also whenever a word can be syllabified in more
than one way. *Webster's Third New International Dictionary*, for
instance, indicates syllable division by using a centered period in the
respelling for pronunciation. Syllable division does not necessarily
coincide with hyphenation which is indicated in this dictionary by
using a centered period in the entry word itself. For example :

met·tric   /me·trik/

Another pronunciation feature which can be indicated when the
whole entry word is transcribed is the primary and secondary stresses
of the word. The above-cited dictionary, for example, employs a high-
set mark, ('), to indicate primary stresses and a low-set mark (ı) to
show secondary stresses. For example :

1. import   /im'pōrt/   (v.)
2. import   /'impōrt/   (n.)

Both marks are used at the same time to indicate stress variations, e.g.

ben·e·fi·cial   /ıbenə:fishəl/

Another aspect of this position is that a word is isolated and its
pronunciation is recorded, as in a list not as joined with other words
in discourse. Although lexicographers are aware of the fact that words

---

[39] Ali M. Al-Kasimi, "Review of Al-Mawrid : A Modern English-Arabic Dictionary,"
in *Papers Presented to Archibald A. Hill by his Students*, ed. by Ali M. Al-Kasimi *et al.*
(Austin, 1971) mimeographed, p. 118.

are normally pronounced with other words in running speech, not in isolation, and that pronunciation provided in the dictionary is not accurate, they stick to their position for practical reasons. Gove says :

> ...it is impracticable to show in a dictionary many kinds of variation —rising or falling pitch, syllabic emphasis or lack of emphasis, contraction or prolongation of sounds—to which the pronunciation of a word is susceptible under the influence of other words temporarily associated with it.[40]

(b) The second position recommends that a minimum of information on pronunciation should be provided in the dictionary. Languages which have "good" phonetic writing systems need not be transcribed at all. Finnish, for example, has an almost complete item-to-item correspondence between sound and spelling; and stress always falls on the first syllable. The exceptions to this item-to-item correspondence between Finnish sound and spelling are very few and can be easily stated in the front matter. Some other languages such as Italian and Modern Turkish have "good" phonetic spelling but stress is not so predictable, therefore it can be indicated on the entry word itself, and there is no need for a respelling. In some other languages, like the Semitic ones whose writing systems do not normally now use vowels, the explicit use of vowels in the dictionary serves as a phonetic clue.[41] In the case of the languages which have "bad" spellings, such as English, stress should be marked on the entry word itself and only that troublesome phoneme of the word should be transcribed. For example :

        lead   (v.)   /iy/
        lead   (n.)   /e/

Yakov Malkiel defends this technique as "most economical, and at the same time, didactically most effective to reduce the phonetic information here to the problem directly involved...."[42]

(c) The third position pertaining to the amount of phonological information should be provided in a bilingual dictionary asserts that not only the entry word should be transcribed but the illustrative examples as well. By adopting this technique, a lexicographer will be able to show the pronunciation of the entry words not in isolation

---

[40] Philip B. Gove, ed., *Webster's Third New International Dictionary of the English Language* (Springfield, Mass. : G. & C. Merriam Co., 1961), p. 7a.

[41] Yakov Malkiel, "Lexicography," in *The Learning of Language*, ed. by Carroll B. Reed (New York : Appleton-Century-Crofts, 1971), p. 371.

[42] *Ibid.*, pp. 370-371.

only, but in running living speech as well. The illustrative examples can be chosen in such a way as to show the entry word under different stress levels, with various pitch patterns, as joined with a neighboring word, and in different positions in the sentence. In this way both segmental and suprasegmental phonemes of the sound system can be indicated in the phonological information provided in the dictionary. Hill, the leading exponent of this position, says :

> The transcription of the word [[fɔ́rnɪtšər]] is a representation of the storage form, and is an abstraction which is never heard. The citation form, which would not be found in the dictionary entry, would be
>
> [fɔ́rnɪtšər]
>
> That is, the citation form would be complete with sentence stress, pitch patterns and terminal pause. The sentence forms of the word are fully exemplified in the illustrations.[43]

The illustration he cites are as follows :

furniture.   [fɔ́rnɪtšər] ...

1. Yesterday we bought furniture and pictures. The furniture was expensive.
[yɛ́stərdiy wibɔ́t fɔ́rnɪtšərən pĭktšərz ⧣ ðəfɔ́rnɪtšərəz ìkspɛ́nsɪv ⧣]

2. Our house doesn't have much furniture.
[àr háws dəzən hæv mɔ́tš fɔ́rnɪtšər ⧣]

3. That store sells a lot of furniture.
[ðǽt stɔ́r sɛ́lzə látə fɔ́rnɪtšər ⧣]

4. We bought three pieces of furniture—a table and two chairs.
[wibɔ́t θríy píysəzə fɔ́rnitšər ⧣ ə téybələn túw tšĕ́rz ⧣]

5. Their furniture astonished their architect.
[ðɛrfɔrnitšər əstáništ ðɛr ǎrkitɛkt ⧣][44]

Examining these three positions in the light of the typology presented in Chapter 2, one can see that the first two techniques might be useful in monolingual dictionaries or bilingual dictionaries for comprehension. The only technique appropriate in a bilingual dictionary for production (especially production of the spoken language) is the one proposed by Hill.

3.1.5 Another question pertaining to phonological information in the bilingual dictionary is, "Which language should be transcribed, the

---

[43] Archibald A. Hill, "Notes on dictionary entries on furniture," mimeographed notes, Univ. of Texas, 1971, p. 3.

[44] *Ibid.*, p. 2.

source or the target?" A survey of a large number of existing commercial bilingual dictionaries illustrates that there is a consistent tradition regarding this issue. Those dictionaries that provide phonological information always give the transcription of the entry words of the source language. This policy does not always serve the dictionary user. Take any English-French dictionary, and you will find that it supplies the pronunciation of the English entry words only. Suppose that this dictionary is used by an American as an aid to produce spoken French. It is obvious, in this case, that its phonological information is useless since he knows the pronunciation of the English words, and the dictionary does not serve that student because it does not provide the pronunciation of the French equivalents. The only way to go around this difficulty according to the traditional approach is to have a bidirectional dictionary (English-French and French-English dictionary) and the American student has to find the French word he wants by using the first half of the dictionary (English-French), then by using the other half (French-English) he can learn the pronunciation of that French lexical item. It should be pointed out in this connection that very few dictionaries are bidirectional, and even if the student had a bidirectional dictionary the method is cumbersome and time consuming.

The best way to solve this problem is to take the new typology (Chapter 2) into account and apply the following formula: If the bilingual dictionary is meant as an aid to the speakers of the source language, then it should furnish phonological information about the target language, and vice versa. Some may object to this technique on the ground that it is expensive. Bilingual dictionaries usually cite several translational equivalents in the target language and to transcribe all these equivalents consumes space. But as we will see in Chapter 3, Section 1, it is advisable to cite one translational equivalent only, and so the objection is met.

3.1.6 A major controversial question pertains to the use of a standard dialect in the dictionary. Although this problem will be discussed in detail in Chapter 5, the present section attempts to shed some light on the term "dialect" and how more than one dialect can be recorded in the dictionary. Modern linguists look at a dialect as a bundle of characteristics peculiar to a language in a specific locality or specific social environment, and not as a deviation from the standard dialect.[45]

---

[45] Arthur J. Bronstein, "The pronunciation of English," in *The Random House*

Dialects can be distinguished in the light of the patterned and systematic linguistic differences which can be correlated with geographical areas and socioeconomic levels.[46] These differences or variations in language show themselves at all levels: in phonology, syntax, semantics, and lexicon. In the words of Sapir:

> A group of dialects is merely the socialized form of the universal tendency to individual variation in speech. These variations affect the phonetic form of the language, its formal characteristics, its vocabulary and such prosodic features as intonation and stress.[47]

To Edward Sapir, a dialect is larger than an idiolect—the characteristic speech of a single speaker—and smaller than a language. The test of mutual intelligibility distinguishes between a language and a dialect. "By reference the term dialect is restricted to a form of speech which does not differ sufficiently from another form of speech to be unintelligible to the speakers of the latter."[48] In each language there are several regional dialects. English, for instance, has American, British, and Scottish. And each regional dialect can be divided into geographical areas. In American English, for example, there are Northern, Midland, and Southern speech.

Within each geographical dialect there are a number of sub-dialects. Hans Kurath distinguishes three defined social variants of speech within any geographical area. These variants are:

(a) *cultivated* speech of urban dwellers who have had college education, wide reading, and many cultural contacts.

(b) *folk* speech of remote or isolated rural dwellers who enjoy little education and few cultural contacts.

(c) *common* speech of the great majority of speakers who have had less education and fewer cultural contacts than the speakers of cultivated speech.[49] From the linguistic point of view there is no "better" dialect except as it facilitates communication in a certain situation.

Dictionary of the English Language, ed. by Jess Stein (New York : Random House, 1966), p. xxiii.

[46] Henry Lee Smith, Jr. "Dialects of English," in *The American Heritage Dictionary of the English Language*, ed. by William Morris (Boston : American Heritage Publishing Co., Inc., 1969), p. xxv.

[47] Edward Sapir, "Dialect," in *English Linguistics*, ed. by Harold Hungerford, Jay Robinson and James Sledd (Glenview, Ill. : Scott, Foresman and Company, 1970), p. 168.

[48] *Ibid.*, p. 169.

[49] Arthur J. Bronstein, *op. cit.*, p. xxiii.

Every speaker is able to use two styles : *formal* and *informal*. In the case of cultivated speech, the formal style is reserved for public speeches, scholarly reports, and the like, whereas the cultivated informal is used on other occasions. Of course, there is a great deal of overlapping between the two styles.

The question that faces the lexicographer is which dialect and which style he should record in his dictionary. Because of limitations on size the lexicographer has to adopt a standard according to which all the vocabulary of the language is pronounced. In other words, the pronunciation presented in the dictionary should represent consistently a selected dialect and a selected style of speech. The traditional approach tends to record the formal style of the cultivated speech. In the introduction to *Webster's Second New International Dictionary*, it is stated that the style of speech represented in the dictionary is that of "formal platform speech," and the words are pronounced in isolation.[50] Linguists question this approach seriously. It is more desirable to have the student speak in a normal way and not to use bookish or "formal platform speech" in casual conversation.[51] Ideally a bilingual dictionary should be confined to one regional dialect and record its phonology, syntax, semantics, and lexicon. In this way the lexicographer will get rid of the labelling of regionalisms which Urdang described as "one of the lexicographer's biggest headaches."[52] If the lexicographer, for one reason or another, wishes to accommodate more than one geographical or social variation, these pronunciation variants should be labeled properly.

Sledd argues that instead of citing all variants of pronunciation in the dictionary, the lexicographer can give one highly abstract underlying form from which all other dialectal pronunciations can be derived by applying the ordered phonetic rules of a transformational grammar which should be listed in the front matter of the dictionary.[53] The application of Sledd's proposal presupposes that dialectologists work out the necessary ordered phonetic rules; this has not been done or completed yet. There is another practical objection to Sledd's doctrine.

---

[50] William Allen Neilson, ed. *Webster's New International*, 2nd Edition, p. xii.

[51] James Sledd, "The lexicographer's uneasy chair," p. 234.

[52] Laurence Urdang, "Review of problems in lexicography," *Language*, 39 (1963), p. 591.

[53] James Sledd, lectures on Lexicography at the University of Texas, Fall 1971. Professor Sledd's proposal is originated and exemplified in his article, "Breaking, umlaut, and the southern drawl," published in *Language*, 42 (1966), pp. 18-41.

The layman dictionary user might not have the time or the skill to apply the suggested rules to the abstract underlying form cited in the dictionary to come out with the pronunciation of the dialect he wanted. If Sledd's doctrine is possible, then this writer suggests that the dictionary should cite the pronunciation of a selected dialect from which other dialectal variations can be derived by applying the phonetic rules stated in the front matter. In this way the layman user of the dictionary has at hand an actual pronunciation which he can use.

3.2   *Morphology and Syntax*

3.2.1   Traditionally, dictionaries provide only minimal information on grammar. Sixty years ago, Steger wrote in a doctoral dissertation on American dictionaries that "the functions of a modern dictionary are in the main, five : to give for each word the correct orthography, syllabification, pronunciation, derivation, and definitions."[54] As is pointed out in this statement, very little grammatical information was given in the dictionaries at that time. Unfortunately, recent dictionaries have not tried to pay better attention to grammar. Instead, they uniformly present limited grammatical information, and most of them do not include a chapter or a section on the grammar of the language in the front matter,[55] although English lexicographic tradition has always demanded that a dictionary should include a grammar and a history of the language in the front matter.[56]

Good dictionaries usually record gender, for those languages which have it, exceptional case forms, irregular plurals, and various conjugations of irregular verbs and point out which of two competing forms is the commoner. They also label by parts of speech, but labelling by parts of speech is usually defective and incomplete. Most dictionaries use the label "noun," for instance, but they fail to indicate the subcategories of this class such as mass noun and count noun.[57] On the syntactic side, the existing dictionaries provide little or no information on matters of word order and clause structure. Malkiel, who examined a large number of Spanish and English dictionaries, says :

---

[54] Stewart A. Steger, *American Dictionaries* (Baltimore : J. H. Furst Co., 1913), p. 1.

[55] Harry R. Warfel, "Dictionaries and linguistics," *College English*, 22 (1961), p. 473.

[56] James Sledd and Gwin J. Kolb, *Dr. Johnson's Dictionary*, p. 12.

[57] Dwight Bolinger, *Aspects of Language* (New York : Harcourt, Brace & World, 1968), p. 290.

Except for a few overworked examples such as *nuevo sombrero* 'newly acquired hat' vs. *sombrero nuevo* 'new-style hat,' the English-speaking student of Spanish will receive on this score severely limited help from his bilingual dictionary. Also he may glean such stray bits of information as that clause openers like *antes (de) que* 'before' and *sin que* 'without' govern the subjunctive (a firm rule) but he is unlikely to learn much about those modal constructions which either allow free choice or demand far narrower rigid rules, as is true of Sp. *despues que* 'after,' *hasta que* 'until,' *mientras (que)* 'while,' etc.[58]

These are just examples of how the morphological and syntactical information provided in the existing dictionaries is defective and incomplete. In short, these dictionaries, as Gleason rightly noted, have failed to present an integrated and adequate linguistic description of the lexicon of the language.[59] But lexicographers claim that it is not feasible to produce a grammar which is completely adequate or satisfactory; consequently the dictionary will not be able to provide the desired integrated linguistic description of the lexicon of the language. In the words of Urdang:

...a completely adequate grammar or dictionary of a living language may not be feasible: perhaps we are imposing on ourselves demands that by their nature never can be met.[60]

As we will see later in this chapter, modern linguists have suggested a number of applicable techniques which can increase and improve the grammatical information in the dictionary.

3.2.2 A dictionary presupposes a grammar, and a lexicographer should have a firm grasp of the morphology and syntax of the language or languages he is dealing with. As Householder put it, lexicographers should "prepare a complete syntactical grammar of their language as a necessary preliminary to writing their dictionary."[61] A bilingual dictionary requires a contrastive grammatical analysis of the source and target languages; then, in the light of the purpose of the dictionary, those morphological and syntactical features in

---

[58] Yakov Malkiel, "Lexicography," p. 372.

[59] H. A. Gleason, Jr., "The relation of lexicon and grammar," in Householder and Saporta, pp. 103.

[60] Laurence Urdang, "Review of Problems in Lexicography," *Language* 39 (1963), p. 592.

[61] Fred W. Householder, Jr., "Lists in grammars," in Logic, *Methodology and Philosophy of Science, Proceedings of the 1960 International Congress* (Stanford, Calif.: Stanford University Press, 1962), p. 576.

which the two languages disagree are chosen for preferential or exclusive listing.[62]

If a policy of selectivity regarding the types of grammatical information is acceptable in a bilingual dictionary for comprehension, a bilingual dictionary for production should include all necessary grammatical information about the target language for two reasons :

(a) to enable the foreign learner to produce adequate sentences in the target language.

(b) to provide the foreign learner with all the information he needs without referring him to handbooks of grammar. As Malkiel pointed out :

> The majority of language learners, who of course share neither the enthusiasm nor the scholarly leisure of professional linguists, are easily irritated by the need to interrupt their readings and go back to a handbook of grammar, ...because this operation is time consuming. The level-headed user's secret wish is to find, at a glance, all the requisite grammatical and lexical assistance wrapped into a single package.[63]

Most linguists probably agree that a dictionary should include a grammar of the foreign language in the front matter. This grammar should outline the morphology and syntax of the language. It should include, for instance, a systematic presentation of derivation, and word-formation. Every language has its own devices for forming derived words from morphemes, such as compounding (composition), suffixation, zero changes (shifting a word from one class to another), and reduplication. Such word-formation habits of the foreign language should be explained in detail in the grammar in order to cut down the need for redundant information in the dictionary (e.g. articles on goodness, wholesomeness, and the like).[64] It should also deal with the distribution of words into classes based on formal signals (e.g. inflectional distinctions) and/or their syntactic behavior (e.g. the positions taken by words in sentences).[65] The grammar in the front matter should also take care of all relationships between classes. It is also important that all subclasses and subcategories be pointed out in that grammar. The grammatical notes in the front matter should be "organized in

---

[62] Yakov Malkiel, "Lexicography," p. 372.

[63] *Ibid.*, p. 371.

[64] Donald C. Swanson, "The selection of entries for a bilingual dictionary," in Householder and Saporta, p. 66.

[65] Kemp Malone, "Structural linguistics and bilingual dictionaries," in Householder and Saporta, p. 118.

such a way as to facilitate the use of the dictionary and give adequate definition of the grammatical identifications which are there given."[66]

The body of the dictionary should serve as an index to the grammar. Each lexical item should be clearly identified, i.e. to which class and subclasses it belongs. In Gleason's words :

> The dictionary should give for each item all pertinent grammatical identification. It is inadequate, particularly in a bilingual dictionary, merely to label items as noun or verb if it is known that there are significant subclasses within such classes. The dictionary should indeed index the grammatical statement.[67]

The dictionary should also function as an amendment to the grammar. If there are two forms which are assigned to the same class in the grammar, but whose distribution is not entirely parallel, the dictionary should state the difference. If an American who is learning French looks up the words "An" and "Année" in any French-English dictionary he will find that both of them are nouns meaning "year" with the exception that the former is masculine and the latter feminine. Therefore he assumes that he can use them interchangeably. And so he has been misled by the dictionary. A good dictionary should amend the grammatical statement and point out the difference in distribution between "An" and "Année." It should state, for example, that *An* is used with cardinal adjectives (exception : tous les ans,) and *Année* is used with ordinal adjectives and expressions of indeterminate quantities and durations. These lexical statements should be exemplified with illustrative examples.

3.2.3   Grammatical information can be implicit in the basic issue of the selection of entries. Traditionally, the entries of the dictionary consist chiefly of individual words and secondarily of idioms. In accord with Bloomfield's definition of lexicon as "a list of basic irregularities," the morpheme, not the word, should be the unit in determining what entries to include in the dictionary, because "every morpheme of a language," explained Bloomfield, "is an irregularity, since the speaker can use it only after hearing it used and the reader of a linguistic description can know of its existence only if it is listed for him."[68] This means that the main entries of the bilingual dictionary should

---

[66] H. A. Gleason, Jr., "The relation of lexicon and grammar," in Householder and Saporta, p. 102.

[67] *Ibid.*

[68] Leonard Bloomfield, *Language*, p. 274.

be devoted to morphemes and morphemic sequences such as (a) bound morphemes (dis-, -ly, etc.), (b) free morphemes and single words (boy, happiness, etc.), (c) multiwords and phrases (carbon paper, jack-in-the-pulpit, used to, etc.).[69' 70] Opinions are split on the usefulness of listing once or twice a binuclear idiom such as "to make sure." The advocates of the single listing are also divided on whether to enter such an idiom under the core word "sure" or under the first element "make."[71] Many dictionaries fail to list idioms under one of their constituents in a consistent way. Thus "by and large" is entered under "by," "at large" under "large;" but "at most" and "at last" are under "at;" and while "on the cheap" is listed under "on," "on the contrary" is entered under "contrary" and so on.[72] To get rid of this confusing procedure, idioms should be listed under each of their constituents [73] with cross references wherever necessary. Irregular forms and alternate spellings such as geese, sang, and caddice should be listed separately from goose, sing, and caddis (though cross-referenced) so that "those who search for them under either form, may not search in vain," as Dr. Johnson noted.[74]

Another grammatical question pertaining to the selection of entries is when to consider two occurrences of a word as one word and when as two words. Traditionally dictionaries lump together homonyms (forms pronounced alike but having different meaning or reference) such as bay_1, adj. "reddish brown," bay_2, n. "inlet of the sea," bay_3, n. "space between columns," bay_4, n. "laurel tree," and bay_5, v. "to bark." Linguists questioned this procedure and recommended that homonyms or homographs (forms spelled alike though sounding different as with "are_1," in "the boys are in here" and "are_2," in "one are equals 100 square meters")[75] should be kept apart in the dictionary, i.e. given separate main entries. Hill formulated the basic principle which should govern such cases as follows:

---

[69] Kemp Malone, "Structural linguistics and bilingual dictionaries," pp. 113-114.

[70] Donald C. Swanson, "The selection of entries for a bilingual dictionary," pp. 64-65.

[71] Yakov Malkiel, "Lexicography," p. 367.

[72] Ali M. Al-Kasimi, "Review of Al-Mawrid: A Modern English-Arabic Dictionary," p. 121.

[73] F. W. Householder, "Summary report," in Householder and Saporta, p. 279.

[74] Samuel Johnson, *Dictionary of the English Language*, p. 5.

[75] The two examples are from *Webster's Third New International Dictionary*, p. 16a.

...differences in sound are significant if they correlate with differences in words or word-elements. Differences in words and word-elements are significant if they correlate with differences in sentences.[76]

A major controversial question pertains to the listing of the several grammatical functions of a single word separately. In other words, if a word like "love" functions as a noun and a verb, should these two parts of speech be treated under the same entry as in *Larousse English-French Dictionary*[77] and the *Random House Dictionary* or as two separate words as in *Webster's Third New International Dictionary?* Urdang criticizes the practice of *Webster's Third* in this connection, and says :

...that practice involves assumptions that require verification from linguistic theory (as well as from etymological facts), and the prefatory matter in the dictionary in question does not contain enough justification for this style.[78]

This practice of listing parts of speech separately was also criticized by Weinreich on the ground that it is not in harmony with "the productiveness of detransitivizing patterns in English" and because it "leads to an uneconomical repetition of definitions."[79] But both objections raised by Weinreich are peculiar to English monolingual dictionaries. A more productive and more general principle based on a sound linguistic theory is needed to be applied to both monolingual and bilingual dictionaries and to cover a larger number of languages. The Hill principle meets these requirements :

We separate words when to do so preserves a rule of syntax which proves useful elsewhere in description of structure.[80]

Consequently, the practice of treating parts of speech separately in the bilingual dictionary can be defended if it is based on this principle which will definitely facilitate learning and result in greater understanding of the structure of the foreign language on the part of the dictionary user.

---

[76] Archibald A. Hill, "Laymen, lexicographers, and linguists," *Language*, 46 (1970), p. 249.

[77] Marguerite-Marie Dubois, *Larousse French-English, English-French Modern Dictionary* (Paris : Librairie Larousse, 1969).

[78] Laurence Urdang, "Review of problems in lexicography," *Language*, 39 (1963), p. 587.

[79] Uriel Weinreich, "Webster's Third : a critique of its semantics," *International Journal of American Linguistics*, 30 (1964), p. 408.

[80] Archibald A. Hill, *op. cit.*, p. 250.

3.2.4 Linguistics can contribute significantly to the grammatical aspect of the dictionary by improving and perfecting the technique of labeling entries according to parts of speech. As has been already pointed out, this technique as it is used now in dictionaries is defective. Here are a few examples of how to improve these labels :

(a) Dictionaries use the label "noun," but they fail to indicate subcategories of this class such as "animate" and "inanimate," and "mass noun" (uncountable) and "count noun." Bolinger noted that *Webster's Third* marks "whim" as a noun and groups it with "caprice" and "fancy," and marks "folly" as a noun and groups it with "indulgence," "vanity," and "foolery." In this case, the dictionary user is not able to tell that "a little whim" refers to something little, whereas "a little indulgence" refers to an amount of indulgence.[81] Such a type of information is certainly valuable in a bilingual dictionary. In this respect, some linguists are not satisfied with marking the entry word as "countable" or "uncountable" only, but they insist that a dictionary intended as an aid to the foreign learner to produce grammatical sentences should supplement that label with explanation and numerous illustrative examples showing the syntactic behavior of the word in question. In his suggested entry on the word "furniture," Hill records the following explanation and illustrative examples :

> FURNITURE. [fərnɪtšər]. Noun, inanimate, pure uncountable.... (To list item of furniture, we enumerate tables, chairs, beds, desks, cabinets. It is noteworthy that the class noun *furniture* is an uncountable but that the items which make up the class are all countable.)
> 1.   Yesterday we bought furniture and pictures. The furniture was expensive.[82]
> 2.   Our house does not have much furniture.
> 3.   That store sells a lot of furniture.
> 4.   We bought three pieces of furniture—a table and two chairs.
> 5.   Their furniture astonished their architect.[83]

Instead of commenting on the usefulness of the labels used and of the illustrative examples cited, it is wiser to quote again Professor Hill's explanation which is stated precisely and neatly :

> The statement that the noun is a 'pure uncountable' means that, at least in this sense, it does not have countable variants, like say, *bread*, which occurs as a countable meaning 'types or brands of bread.'

---

[81] Dwight Bolinger, *Aspects of Language*, p. 290.

[82] The phonemic transcription of the illustrative examples is deleted from the quotation.

[83] Archibald A. Hill, "Notes on dictionary entries on *furniture*," p. 2.

The sentences illustrate the characteristics of an uncountable, that is, the absence of a plural and indefinite article, the use of itemizers and quantifiers (*piece*, and *a lot of*), and the use of *much* instead of *many* with a negative.

The fact that the noun is inanimate means that, unless there is personification, the noun cannot be used with verbs which ascribe internal emotional or intellectual states to it. That is, we cannot say '*The furniture was astonished.' The same applies to adjectives, since we cannot say '*That is cowardly furniture.'[84]

In a dictionary of a smaller size the number of illustrative examples can be reduced if the characteristics of the uncountable and inanimate nouns are stated in the grammar in the front matter.

Gender should also be indicated in the bilingual dictionary which deals with languages that have it such as Arabic, French, and Spanish. Whereas an English noun is labeled as (n.), an Arabic one should be marked as (m.) "masculine," (f.) "feminine," or (s.) "both masculine and feminine."

(b) Dictionaries label adjectives but they fail to indicate further information about this class. The following are some useful pieces of information that should be furnished in the bilingual dictionary :

(i) comparison : It must be made clear whether an adjective is compared with -*er* and -*est* (big, bigger, biggest), with *more* and *most* (beautiful, more beautiful, most beautiful), has irregular comparative forms (little, less, least), or does not belong to any of the three previous subcategories, such as "initial," "seismic," and "annual," which do not have comparative forms.[85]

(ii) The order classes : In a noun phrase where there are no separators other than pluses, adjectives occur according to fixed rules of order. Every adjective entered in the dictionary should be labeled as to its relative position in the noun phrase. Hill numbers the words of a noun phrase according to their closeness to the head of the phrase, the noun. His model noun phrase is :

VI V   IV III II   I   N
all the ten fine old stone houses.[86]

Hill provides the following rules which govern the assigning of adjectives to the same or different order classes :

---

[84] *Ibid.*, p. 3.
[85] Dwight Bolinger, *Aspects of Language*, p. 291.
[86] Archibald A. Hill, *Introduction to Linguistic Structures*, p. 176.

Two words belong to the same order class if one can substitute for the other without affecting the framework of the phrase. Two words belong to different order classes either if they occur in a fixed sequence, as do *the* and *ten*, or if their sequence can be broken only by placing a terminal juncture between them. Finally, two words belong to the same order class if they can occur in the order AB or BA, but require a terminal, A/B or B/A, between them, as do *old* and *gray*.[87]

(iii) prenominality: The dictionary should indicate whether an adjective is prenominal, postnominal or both. "Content," for instance, is a postnominal adjective, and so we can say "the men are content," but not "*the content men." On the other hand, "late" in "John Kennedy, the late President, ..." is a prenominal only; we cannot say "the President is late" with the same meaning. Other adjectives are both prenominal and postnominal; e.g. "happy" appears in "the man is happy" and "he is a happy man." Hill recommended that a serious attempt should be undertaken to survey English adjectives and differentiate between these three subcategories.[88]

(c) Dictionaries label verbs as transitive or intransitive, but they fail to indicate their other categories such as :

(i) saturated and unsaturated verbs : Bolinger suggests that verbs, whether intransitive or transitive with an expressed object, should be divided into the subcategories of *saturated* and *unsaturated*. The former refers to the verbs that do not require something further to complete them, e.g. "I *saddled* the horse." The latter designated verbs which require something further than their object to complete them, e.g. "*I *saddled* him" (which needs, for example, "with responsibilities").[89]

(ii) case government : Dictionaries should indicate whether a prepositional phrase which completes a transitive verb is obligatory or optional. In the sentences

I put the car *in the garage*.
I washed the car *in the garage*.

the prepositional phrase in the first is obligatory while it is optional in the second.[90] As Weinreich rightly noted:

---

[87] *Op. cit.*

[88] Archibald A. Hill, "The promises and limitations of the newest type of grammatical analysis," *TESOL Quarterly*, 1 (1967), pp. 16-17.

[89] Dwight Bolinger, *op. cit.*, p. 292.

[90] Henry M. Hoenigswald, "Lexicography and grammar," in Householder and Saporta, p. 109.

The failure to distinguish between the essential and the optional, together with the neglect to specify the prohibited, deprives the dictionary, as a descriptive instrument, of any generative power. In calling a statement 'generative,' we mean that it is literally applicable to all the phenomena it subsumes, and to no other.[91]

(iii) The dictionary should mark those pure intransitive verbs that "have the ability to occur with complements, if the complement is cognate in form and meaning with verb,"[92] such as *die* and *laugh* in :

He died.
He died *a hero's death*.
He laughed.
He laughed *a loud laugh*.

(iv) Hill reminded lexicographers of a subcategory of the transitive verb which was set up by Jespersen who called it the "move-change class," "the characteristics of which were that there could be an animate subject with an inanimate complement, as in 'John moved a chair;' but if the animate subject was absent, the complement could become the new subject, as in 'the chair moved.'"[93]

(d) Adverbs can be also classified into subclasses according to the part of the sentences which the adverb modifies :

(i) adverbs which modify forms of verbs but not adjectives; e.g. *well*-bred, *fast*-disappearing (not *well white).

(ii) adverb which modify adjectives or adverbs, but not verbs; e.g. *very* new, *very* quickly (not *to speak very). Notice that in "*very* excited," "excited" is an adjective and no longer a verb.

(iii) adverbs which modify sentences; e.g. *usually* it does.

(iv) adverbs which can join verbs to make idioms, e.g. leave *out* the details; other adverbs cannot; e.g. *leave *quickly* the city.[94]

The above cited categories are just examples to illustrate the fact that labeling by parts of speech can be immensely improved if linguistic studies are taken into consideration by lexicographers.

---

[91] Uriel Weinreich, "Webster's Third : A critique of its semantics," p. 407.
[92] Archibald A. Hill, "Laymen, lexicographers, and linguists," p. 250.
[93] *Ibid.*, p. 251.
[94] Dwight Bolinger, *op. cit.*, p. 291.

CHAPTER FOUR

SEMANTIC PROBLEMS IN THE BILINGUAL DICTIONARY

4.0 The semantic problems involved in bilingual dictionaries are different from and more complicated than those in monolingual ones because the latter are prepared for people who participate and understand the culture being described whereas the former describe a culture which differs, in various proportions, from the users'.[1] Like other aspects of linguistic description, semantic studies have not always been appreciated by lexicographers. As Nida noted :

> An essential part of investigations in semantics is reflected in dictionary-making, a highly specialized process, which, however, too often reflects only a meager appreciation of some fundamental problems involved in the analysis of meaning.[2]

This chapter is an attempt to shed light on only three semantic problems involved in bilingual lexicography and to suggest possible solutions. The three problems are : the choice of equivalents, meaning discrimination, and word family.

4.1 *The Choice of Equivalents*

4.1.1 The major task of a bilingual lexicographer is to find appropriate equivalents in the target language to the units of the source language. This task involves a great deal of translation. Jakobson labels differently three kinds of translation :

> 1) intralingual translation or *rewording* is an interpretation of verbal signs by means of other signs of the same language.
> 2) interlingual translation or *translation proper* is an interpretation of verbal signs by means of some other language.
> 3) intersemiotic translation or transmutation is an interpretation of verbal signs by means of signs of nonverbal sign systems.[3]

Bilingual lexicography is obviously concerned with translation proper or interlingual translation which will be referred to here as "trans-

---

[1] Eugene A. Nida, "Analysis of meaning and dictionary making," *International Journal of American Linguistics*, 24 (1958), p. 279.

[2] *Ibid.*

[3] Roman Jakobson, "On linguistic aspects of translation," in *On Translation*, ed. by Reuben A. Brower (Cambridge, Mass. : Harvard Univ. Press, 1959), p. 233.

lation." There are various ways to define translation, but all definitions share one or more of the following concepts depending upon the special interest of each writer :[4]

(a) The transference of meaning from one text to another language. An example of this concept is Dostert's definition of translation as "the branch of applied science of language which is specifically concerned with the problem—or the fact—of the transference of meaning from one set of patterned symbols ... into another set of patterned symbols."[5]

(b) Transcoding or the transformation of symbols. This concept is represented by Oettinger's definition of translation in terms of "the process of transforming signs or representation into another signs or representation."[6]

(c) Finding equivalent lexical items. Oettinger's definition of interlingual translation as "the replacement of elements of one language, the domain of translation, by equivalent elements of another language, the range,"[7] serves as an example here.

Although a bilingual dictionary deals mainly with the last concept, namely the translation of entry words, the other two concepts are also relevant as in the translation of the illustrative sentences and in transliteration of proper nouns of the source language for which there is no possible translation in the target language, especially when the two languages employ different writing systems.

4.1.2 Whereas a monolingual lexicographer deals with defining equivalents, his bilingual counterpart is specifically concerned with translation equivalents. Broadly speaking, a translation-equivalent can be defined as "a target-language text, or item-in-text which changes when and only when a given source-language text or item is changed."[8] One of the linguistic processes to establish translation-equivalents is the commutation test which makes use of a bilingual as an informant. The bilingual is presented with a sentence in the source language and requested to put it in the target language. Then the items of the sentence are gradually changed one by one and every time an item is changed

---

[4] J. C. Catford, "Translation and language teaching," in *Linguistic Theories and Their Application* (London : AIDELA, 1967), p. 126.

[5] Dostert as quoted in J. C. Catford, *op. cit.*

[6] Anthony G. Oettinger, *Automatic Language Translation*, Harvard Monographs in Applied Science No. 8 (Cambridge, Mass. : Harvard University Press, 1960), p. 104.

[7] *Ibid.*, p. 110.

[8] J. C. Catford, "Translation and language teaching," p. 130.

the bilingual provides the proper translation. Catford cites the following example :

> ...I might present my bilingual with the English sentence, 'I bought this book yesterday' and ask for a translation. He supplies 'J'ai acheté ce livre hier.' I then change an item in the source text, and say 'I bought this paper yesterday.' Next [the] bilingual supplies 'J'ai acheté ce journal hier.' Next I supply 'I bought these papers yesterday' and receive the translation 'J'ai acheté ces journaux hier.' In this way I establish the translation-equivalence of *book* = livre, *paper* = journal, *this paper* = ce journal, *these papers* = ces journaux, etc.[9]

Nida recommends that even if a lexicographer has long experience with the foreign language he should seek the constant help of a native informant of that language in order to weed out improper usage and avoid translationisms.[10]

The translations of entry words in a bilingual dictionary are usually of two types : (a) translational equivalents, and (b) explanatory equivalents. A translational equivalent is a lexical unit which can be immediately inserted into a sentence in the target language; e.g. in an English-French dictionary, boy = garçon. An explanatory or descriptive equivalent is one which cannot be always inserted into a sentence in the target language; e.g. boyhood : état de garçon. To cite a translational equivalent for the word "boyhood," the lexicographer may give "adolescence" or "jeunesse." But the English entry word is restricted to male children whereas the two French translational equivalents are not; and so the lexicographer may try a compromise and say, for instance,

> boyhood : adolescence (d'un garçon).[11]

The difference between an explanatory equivalent and an explanation is that whereas the latter tends to be similar to a definition or description, the former tends to approximate a translational unit and so it might be standardized by acceptance and use in the language.[12] Zgusta provides the following example :

> Ossetic Ziw : "Collective help" (socially expected help, above all in agricultural works, or organized within or by a group of people).

---

[9] *Ibid.*

[10] Eugene A. Nida, *Bible Translating* (London : United Bible Societies, 1961), p. 27.

[11] Ladislav Zgusta, "Equivalents and explanations in bilingual dictionaries," a paper presented to the Conference on Lexicography, LSA, Columbus, Ohio, July 23, 1970, pp. 7-8.

[12] *Ibid.*, pp. 10-11.

Here, "collective help" is an explanatory equivalent, and the phrase in parentheses is an explanation. However, Zgusta admits that there are a great number of borderline cases. Nevertheless, the distinction between translational and explanatory equivalents is a useful one. The explanatory equivalent is of a general nature and it works well if the target language is the user's native tongue, because it (the explanatory equivalent) may suggest or elicit in him some other equivalent which fits the particular context he is dealing with. On the other hand, although a translational equivalent conveys less information than an explanatory one, it has the advantage of offering the user a lexical unit which can be directly employed. Consequently, translational equivalents should be favored in a bilingual dictionary intended for the speakers of the source language as an aid to produce the target language.

4.1.3   A major problem which confronts the bilingual lexicographer is that he does not always find the required equivalents in the target language. Two types of vocabulary particularly contribute to this problem : (a) the culture-bound words which denote objects peculiar to the culture of the source language, and (b) the scientific and technological terminology which does not exist in the vernacular languages of the developing countries. Although many of these developing countries have a special linguistic body that undertakes the responsibility of creating the needed vocabulary, the lexicographer and his assistants often find themselves obliged to create a translation equivalent which does not exist in the target language.

The UNESCO committee that studied the use of vernacular languages in education pointed out that there are five different ways to expand or extend a vocabulary : (1) word borrowing, (2) coinage, (3) giving new meaning to existing words, (4) extending the meaning of existing words, and (5) compounding new words from existing elements from the language or from it and some other one. The committee also recommended that devices (3), (4), and (5) should be preferred to (1) and (2), that borrowed words should be adapted to the sound system and grammar of the language, that borrowed scientific terms should be consistent as to the type of information and language of origin, and that the acceptability of all new words should be first tested before they are finally adopted.[13] As Bull pointed out, the use

[13] William E. Bull, "The use of vernacular languages in education," in *Language in Culture and Society*, ed. by Dell Hymes (New York : Harper & Row, Publishers, 1964), p. 530.

of one device or another depends on the subject matter. Political terminology, for instance, can be created by (3), (4), or (5), but the only devices to create a complete pharmacopoeia are borrowing and coinage.[14] Borrowing is often resisted by the purists in the developing countries. The linguistic controversy between the innovators and the purists in many of these countries is similar to that which was going on in the 16th century in England.[15] The innovators defend the practice of free borrowing and adaptation from foreign languages to meet the ever-increasing need for scientific and technical terminology, and the purists protest against the foreign-derived words and urge freer use of pure items taken from the vernacular.

Whatever devices the lexicographer employs to create the closest equivalence in translation, he should take into consideration the three basic requirements which were stated by Nida as follows :

> (1) the translation must represent the customary usage of the receptor language, (2) the translation must make sense, and (3) the translation must conform to the meaning of the original.[16]

4.1.4   Most linguists would agree that "all cognitive experience and its classification is conveyable in any existing language."[17] They would also "reject the idea of the inefficiency, formlessness, and over-particularity of primitive speech..."[18] But whereas it is nearly always possible to establish translation equivalence between sentences, it is often difficult to do so between lexical items.[19] This difficulty rises from the fact that there is a close relationship between language and culture, and since words are "symbols for dynamic and explicit features of the culture,"[20] it is not easy to establish absolute correspondence between related words in two different languages. Cultural differences are explicit, for instance, in words related to ecology, kinship, technologies, currencies, weights and measures, time units, and the like. The difficulty also rises from the very nature of meaning. Nida expressed

---

[14] *Op. cit.*

[15] De Witt T. Starnes and G. E. Noyes, *The English Dictionary from Cawdrey to Johnson* (Chapel Hill : The Univ. of North Carolina Press, 1946), p. 8.

[16] Eugene A. Nida, *Bible Translating* (London : United Bible Societies, 1961), p. 13.

[17] Roman Jakobson, "Linguistic aspects of translation," in *On Translation*, ed. by Reuben A. Brower (Cambridge, Mass. : Harvard Univ. Press, 1959), p. 234.

[18] Archibald A. Hill, "A note on primitive languages," *International Journal of American Linguistics*, 18 (1952), p. 172.

[19] J. C. Catford, "Translation and language teaching," p. 133.

[20] Eugene A. Nida, "Analysis of meaning and dictionary making," p. 282.

the fluid and inconstant nature of meaning of words in his three fundamental semantic presuppositions :

> (1) No word (or semantic unit) ever has exactly the same meaning in two different utterances; (2) there are no complete synonyms within a language; (3) there are no exact correspondences between related words in different languages.[21]

Aside from the differences in connotation and stylistic affiliations, synonyms or near synonyms differ in phonology; there are significant differences in the number of syllables, pattern of stresses, and rhyme.[22]

Absolute equivalents which have exactly the same semantic and grammatical function in both languages are rare. The following are a few examples of why differences between two related items in two languages may exist :

(a) Languages differ in their related grammatical categories.[23] The meaning of the grammatical category "plural" in Arabic, for example is different from its counterpart in English. Arabic has a three-term number system (Singular—Dual—Plural) whereas English has a two-term number system (Singular—Plural). Gender is another example of a grammatical category which differs from one language to another. In Arabic, for instance, "moon" is masculine and "sun" is feminine, but in French the case is reversed.

(b) Languages differ in their parts of speech. Whereas English and many other Indo-European languages traditionally have eight parts of speech, some languages have only three : nouns, verbs, and particles. Languages do not only differ in the number of classes, but in the classification of the same action or state as well. Such English nouns as "food," "faith," and "love" must be translated as verbs in the Mazatec language of Mexico.[24]

(c) A lexical unit in one language may not even have a corresponding lexical unit in another language. The meaning of that lexical unit might be expressed by a syntactical device in the other language. The Arabic word /hal/ has a lexical equivalent in Persian /'āyā/, but it does not have one in English. Its meaning corresponds to a meaning conveyed in English by S-V inversion. E.g. :

'arrajulu ṭawīl.	The man is tall.
hali rrajulu ṭawīl?	Is the man tall?

---

[21] *Ibid.*, p. 281.

[22] H. A. Gleason, Jr. *Linguistics and English Grammar* (New York : Holt, Rinehart and Winston, Inc., 1965), p. 429.

[23] Roman Jakobson, *op. cit.*, pp. 236-237.

[24] Eugene A. Nida, *Bible Translating*, pp. 15-16.

(d) Two different languages may have two different grammatical patterns to determine certain aspects of experience. In order to produce an accurate translation of the English sentence "I met my friend," into Arabic, for example, we have to make our choice between a masculine and feminine noun (ṣadīq or ṣadīqa). This bit of information is considered to be irrelevant in English. On the other hand, when an Arabic verbal sentence is translated into English, some supplementary information is needed. "Waṣala," for example, is either "he arrived" or "he has arrived."[25]

(e) A lexical item may have a proper denotative meaning in one language, but its corresponding item in another language might have undesirable connotations. Vulgarity is not necessarily related to sex and procreation only; in some languages calling one's grandmother by name is considered to be vulgar.[26]

(f) A lexical unit in one language may have two components, like the German greeting "Guten Tag," but its equivalent in another language may have one component only, as in English, where it is translated into a single word, "Hello."[27]

(g) Two related items in two different languages may not cover the same semantic range. The Arabic word "'iṣba'" stands for both "finger" and "toe." On the other hand, the English word "uncle" is the usual translation of the Arabic words "'am" (paternal uncle) and "xāl" (maternal uncle).

4.1.5 The search for equivalents should be preceded by a contrastive analysis of the source and target languages in order to determine the ranks in a grammatical hierarchy (e.g. sentence—clause—group—word —morpheme), to determine corresponding grammatical categories (e.g. plurality, gender, etc.), and to determine reciprocal parts of speech. Usually an English equivalent of a German noun will first be sought among English nouns. But there are exceptions to this principle. Zgusta provides the following example:

> ...German *handarbeit* (subst.) has a good equivalent in English *hand-work* (subst.), but if it is used as a label on wares, the English equivalent is *hand-made*, because the English substantive denotes only the process, not its results.[28]

---

[25] Roman Jakobson, *op. cit.*, pp. 235-236.
[26] Eugene A. Nida, *Bible Translating*, p. 18.
[27] Ladislav Zgusta, *op. cit.*
[28] *Ibid.*, pp. 1-2.

It should be noted that the substantives and adjectives of the target language cannot always be considered as equivalents to the substantives and adjectives of the source language. Whereas an Arabic noun and its related adjectives usually differ in their form, it is not always like that in English where the same word may function as a noun and adjective. E.g. :

(a)	ṣūf	(n) :	wool
	ṣūfī	(a) :	woolen
(b)	ṣaxr	(n) :	stone
	ṣaxrī	(a) :	stone

An Arabic-English dictionary prepared for the speakers of Arabic should not leave English adjectives of type (b) without some indication of how they are used—by citing illustrative phrases, (e.g. stone wall, stone age).[29] When a grammatical category exists in the source language but is absent in the target language, its meaning can be translated by a lexical item. Arabic, for example, has duals but English does not, therefore such Arabic words as /ʾalʿeynān/ should be translated into "the (two) eyes" in an Arabic-English dictionary.[30]

After the contrastive grammatical analysis has been done, the lexicographer has to determine the meanings of the grammatical and lexical items. The analyst should look for the distinctive situational features which are shared by the two related items. The two equivalents must be related to all or some of the same features of the situation.

> ...Among the situational features which may be relevant to the source-language text are those which determine the selection of a particular variety—a particular dialect, register, or style—of the source language.[31]

The lexicographer can follow a certain procedure to determine whether the equivalent he chooses is absolute (i.e. covers the whole range of the lexical meaning of the entry word) or not. He collects a broad range of typical contexts in the source language in which the entry word occurs. Then he translates these sentences into the target language. If the prospective equivalent can fit in each instance of the translated sentence, then it is absolute, otherwise it is partial. In the latter case, the lexicographer has to find some other (partial) equivalent(s).[32] When a partial equivalent is given, the dictionary user's attention must be attracted to the differences, grammatical or semantic.

---

[29] *Ibid.*, p. 2.
[30] Roman Jakobson, *op. cit.*, p. 235.
[31] J. C. Catford, "Translation and language teaching," p. 140.
[32] Ladislav Zgusta, *op. cit.*, p. 3.

If a transitive verb in the source language is given an equivalent which is also transitive, the user may assume that the parallelism between the two words is complete when it is not; and so the bilingualism of dictionaries may become "a dangerous source of unsystematic omission."[33]

The translation of exocentric expressions (idioms and figures of speech) presents special difficulties in bilingual lexicography. Certain types of adaptation are necessary in the translation of these expressions. A metaphor, for example, is not necessarily translated by a corresponding metaphor; it may be translated by a metaphor, a simile, or just a lexical item. If the speakers of the target language have not heard of Adam and they do not grow apples, the English metaphor "Adam's apple" cannot be translated into a metaphor. Metaphors are closely related to the speakers' experience, and when they are translated literally the lexicographer should use certain practical or linguistic devices to attract the user's attention to the fact that the expression involves an unusual extension of meaning, because such extensions of meaning in the source language do not always have parallels in the target language.[34] The bilingual dictionary should also indicate the required preposition which is used with the verb in question, and use some convention to distinguish it from that preposition which forms a part of an idiom. For example, the Arabic verb "'allaqa" (to hang) might be followed by "'alā" (on) either as a preposition or as an adverbial particle. The verb can be entered as follows :

'allaqa ('alā) :   hang (on)
'allaqa 'alā :   comment on

Existing bilingual dictionaries tend to pile up synonyms or near synonyms in the target language. There are two arguments for this trend : (a) it provides the user with various expressions for stylistic variation, and (b) since there are always slight differences between near synonyms, the more synonyms you give the richer the information will be. However, modern linguists prefer to cite one equivalent if possible and to avoid piling up synonyms.[35] As Martin pointed out :

> We want to boil our material down to essentials. In the interest of
> conciseness, we should aim at a single translational equivalent whenever

---

[33] Henry M. Hoenigswald, "Lexicography and grammar," in Householder and Saporta, p. 109.

[34] Eugene A. Nida, *Toward a Science of Translating* (Leiden : E. J. Brill, 1964), pp. 219-220.

[35] Ladislav Zgusta, *op. cit.*, p. 6.

possible. If several equivalents are presented, some indication should be given of the context (or kind of context) that would provoke the less expected version. Our choice of THE equivalent (or the first equivalent) will be determined by the decision which one is more broadly applicable; it should be the particular equivalent that the student is most likely to need.[36]

Ideally the translation-equivalent should stand by itself. Adaptations or comments are never added except in limited cases such as : (a) to avoid ambiguity as in the case of homonyms, (b) to point out that the equivalent is partial and to indicate linguistic or cultural differences between the entry word and its equivalent, and (c) to avoid foreseeable grammatical complications.[37] An example of necessary cultural comments is in *Larousse English-French Dictionary* :

> lunch.... m. lunch, luncheon...
> —N.B. Lunch in French is a meal composed of sandwiches and petit fours, and taken generally standing, at the counter at any hour of the day. It is not the equivalent of the English «lunch».[38]

4.2 *Meaning discrimination*[39]

4.2.1 When a person wants to say something in a foreign language he might consult a bilingual dictionary. But instead of finding one word which expresses his meaning, he is frequently confronted with several words which he cannot distinguish one from another. For example, if a French student of English wants to say "Je vais faire un tour en Angleterre" in English and does not know the equivalent of "tour" in English, he consults a dictionary which may give him the following entry :

> (1) tour... n.m. Turn, round, twining, winding; revolution, circumference, circuit, compass; twist, strain; tour, trip; trick, dodge, wile; feat; office, service, vein, manner; style; place, order; lathe; turning-box; wheel; mould...[40]

And so he will not be able to select the equivalent which fits his meaning unless he has command of the English language, in which

---

[36] Samuel E. Martin, "Selection and presentation of ready equivalents in a translation dictionary," in Householder and Saporta, p. 156.

[37] Yakov Malkiel, "A typological classification of dictionaries on the basis of distinctive features," in Householder and Saporta, p. 15.

[38] Marguerite-Marie Dubois, ed. *Larousse Modern Dictionary*, p. 427.

[39] Most of the examples presented in this section are provided by Janes E. Iannucci and Edwin B. Williams in their six articles listed in the bibliography.

[40] Ernest A. Baker, *Heath's New French & English Dictionary* (Boston : D. C. Heath & Co., 1932).

case it is not too likely that he will need the dictionary.[41] The bilingual dictionary should provide meaning discriminations which enable the user to select the appropriate equivalent or the proper sense of an equivalent. And unless the problem of meaning discrimination is solved systematically, the bilingual dictionary cannot be a dependable guide to the proper equivalents. Meaning discrimination, which is considered by some as "the crucial problem of bilingual lexicographical methodology,"[42] has not yet been completely solved. Williams, who did extensive research on this issue and came out with some successful solutions, admitted that "there are still other aspects of the problem that need to be considered on the basis of further research."[43] This section discusses the types of meaning discrimination, when they should be used, and in which language they should be provided. The section also proposes new formulas which govern the use of meaning discriminations.

4.2.2 There are cases in which a polysemous source (or target) word requires meaning discriminations and there are others in which it does not. The necessity of meaning discrimination depends on the purpose of the dictionary, i.e. whether it is meant for comprehension or production, and whether it is intended for the speaker of the source or the target language.

If the dictionary is prepared for the purpose of production (for the speakers of the source language of course), e.g. an English-Spanish dictionary for English-speaking users, then no meaning discrimination is necessary in the following two cases :

(a) If the source word has one meaning for which the target language has one word of only one meaning. E.g. :

   (2) mosque   S   mezquita

(b) If the source word has one meaning for which the target language has a polysemous word (having two or more meanings). E.g. :

   (3) Tunis   S   Tunez

But meaning discrimination is necessary in the following two cases :

(c) The source word is polysemous and for each of its meanings the target language has a separate word of one meaning. E.g. :

   (4) suicide   S   (act) suicidio; (person) suicida

[41] Mario Pei, *The Story of Language* (Philadelphia, 1949), p. 427.

[42] James E. Iannucci, "Meaning discrimination in bilingual dictionaries: a new lexicographical technique," *Modern Language Journal*, XLI (1957), p. 272.

[43] Edwin B. Williams, "Analysis of the problem of meaning discrimination in Spanish and English bilingual lexicography," *Babel*, 6 (1960), p. 121.

(d) The source word is polysemous and for each of its meanings the target language has two or more polysemous words. E.g. :

   (5) race   S   (contest of speed) carrera;
                           (subdivision of mankind) raza.

If the dictionary is intended for comprehension only (for the speakers of the target language of course); e.g. a Spanish-English dictionary for English-speaking users, then no meaning discrimination is necessary in the following two cases :

(e) The source word has one meaning for which the target language has one word of only one meaning. E.g. :

   (6) mezquita   S   mosque.

(f) The source word is polysemous and for each of its senses the target language has one word of only one meaning. E.g. :

   (7) Tunez   S   Tunis;   Tunisia.

But meaning discrimination is necessary in the following two cases :

(g) The source word has one meaning for which the target language has a polysemous equivalent. E.g. :

   (8) suicidio   m   suicide (act)

(h) The source word is polysemous and for each of its senses the target language has two or more polysemous words. E.g. :

   (9) carrera   f   run (running place);
                           race (contest of speed).

Iannucci thinks that no meaning discrimination is necessary in (g) because the native speaker of the target language is able to select the proper sense of the polysemous target word which fits the source context best.[44] On the other hand, Williams feels that meaning discrimination is necessary in this case "only where the meaning cannot be determined from the context."[45] However, the writer of this book believes that the context does not always help the user select the proper sense of a polysemous equivalent, and the lexicographer has no control over the context, i.e. he cannot tell when the user needs meaning discrimination and when he does not. And since a bilingual dictionary should aim at a maximum utility, it should provide meaning discrimination consistently in (g) as well as in (c), (d), and (h).

---

[44] James E. Iannucci, *op. cit.*, pp. 272-273.
[45] Edwin B. Williams, *op. cit.*, p. 122.

4.2.3 Meaning discrimination can be achieved by the use of one of the following devices :

(a) punctuation : Traditionally dictionaries use punctuation as a kind of negative discrimination. Synonyms or near synonyms are separated by commas, and different meanings by semicolons, as in example (1). This method might be of limited help where meaning discrimination is not needed, as in example (7), but it is of no help at all if it is used by itself where meaning discrimination is necessary.

(b) definitions : Older dictionaries give long formal definitions to discriminate the meanings of a polysemous word. E.g. :

> (10) Spring, s. .... 4. Primavera, estación del año en la cual comienzan las plantas á brotar y crecer...[46]

In another dictionary,[47] this definition is shortened to "estación del año." As a matter of fact, one can cut it down to "estación" alone which will easily serve as a meaning discrimination.[48]

(c) synonyms : Synonyms can provide briefer meaning discriminations. Each target word can be accompanied by one of the synonyms of the polysemous entry word. E.g. :

> (11) nett .... I. (zierlich) elegant, (sauber) neat, tidy, (hübsch) pretty, good-looking, (schmuck, geputzt) smart, trim, (niedlich) nice, delicate, (allerliebst) charming, (gemütlich) jolly, (freudlich) pleasant, (liebenswürdig) amiable, lovable, ...[49]

(d) illustrative examples : Illustrative phrases or sentences may serve as another device of meaning discrimination. E.g. :

> (12) Spring... s. l(a) Source f. (d'eau)... (b) Source, origine f. The custom has its s. in another country, usage a eu son origine dans un autre pays... 2. Printemps m. The glory of an English s., la splendeur du printemps en Angleterre... A lovely s. evening, une belle soirée de printemps. Spring is in the air, on respire le printemps dans l'air ....[50]

It is obvious that this method is space-consuming. Besides, if illustrative examples are not used efficiently and effectively, they will be useless.

---

[46] M. Valazques de la Cadena, *A New Pronouncing Dictionary of the Spanish & English Languages* (Chicago : Wilcox & Follett Co., 1953).

[47] Arturo Cyuas, *Appleton's Revised English-Spanish & Spanish-English Dictionary*, 4th ed. (New York : Appleton-Century-Crofts, Inc., 1953).

[48] James E. Ianucci, "Meaning discrimination in bilingual dictionaries," in Householder and Saporta, p. 202.

[49] *Muret-Sanders Encyclopaedic English-German & German-English Dictionary*, 5th ed. (Berlin : Langenscheidtsche Verlagsbuchhandlung, n.d.).

[50] J. E. Mansion, *Heath's Standard French & English Dictionary*, 2nd ed. (Boston : D. C. Heath & Co., 1939).

(e) parts of speech : Another device of meaning discrimination is the designation of the part of speech of the polysemous entry word. E.g. :

(13) after *adv.* depois, en seguide; *conj.* depois que; *prep.* depois, apos; conforme; segundo....[51]

(f) usage labels : Labeling by usage (e.g. fig., colloq., etc.) and by fields of knowledge (e.g. botany, architecture, etc.) may serve as a device of meaning discrimination. E.g. :

(14) bay ... s. Bahia, cala, rada, ensenada; (bot.) laurel; ladrido, aullido; acorralanieto; pajar; (arq.) intercolumnio; crujia; nave; ....[52]

But since only a limited number of words can be assigned to special fields or usage, this device can only be incidental.

(g) context words or phrases : Any word or phrase which gives only enough of the context in which a polysemous word is usually used may serve as a meaning discrimination :

(i) the subject or type of subject may discriminate the meanings of a verb. E.g. :

(15) Sway .... v.i. (a) balancer; osciller, ballotter; (of drunkard) vaciller; (of trees) To s. in the wind, se balancer au vent... (c) (of balance, etc.) pencher; incliner....[53]

(ii) the object or type of object may discriminate the meanings of a verb also. E.g. :

(16) brocher... v. a. to stitch (a book); to figure (stuffs); to emboss (linen); to strike (a nail into a horse's foot)....[54]

(iii) the noun or type of noun may serve as a context word to discriminate the adjective which qualifies it. E.g. :

(17) dim ... a. ... (of light) faible, pale; (of colour) efface; (of sight) faible; (of memory) uncertain, vague....[55]

(iv) the adjective or type of adjective may serve as a context word to discriminate the noun. E.g. :

(18) journal[1] ... 2. Journal; feuille (quotidienne)....[56]

---

[51] E.L. Richardson, M. de L. Sa Pereira, M. Sa Pereira, *Modern Portuguese-English & English-Portuguese Dictionary* (London: G.G. Harrap & Co., Ltd., 1944).

[52] E.M. Martinez Amador, *Shorter Spanish-English & English-Spanish Dictionary* (Boston : D.C. Heath & Co., 1953).

[53] J.E. Mansion, *Heath's Standard French & English Dictionary.*

[54] Ernest A. Baker, *Cassell's French-English & English-French Dictionary,* 5th ed. (New York : Funk & Wagnalls Co., 1951).

[55] J.E. Mansion, *Mansion's Short French & English Dictionary* (Boston : D.C. Heath & Co., 1940).

[56] J.E. Mansion, *Harrap's Standard French & English Dictionary Part 2 : English-French* (London : Harrap & Co., 1956).

Any of the above-mentioned devices may serve as a meaning discrimination. It goes without saying that the briefer discriminations, such as context words, are preferable because space is an essential practical and economic consideration in lexicography.

4.2.4 A major question pertaining to meaning discrimination is: "In which language should meaning discrimination be presented?" Examining a large number of existing bidirectional dictionaries, one finds that they do not follow a consistent policy in this regard. There are four distinct approaches to the problem:

(a) Meaning discriminations are presented in the target language in both sides of the bidirectional dictionary, as in the fourth edition of Arturo Cuyas's *Appleton's Revised English-Spanish and Spanish-English Dictionary*. And so they are in Spanish in the English-Spanish part and in English in the Spanish-English part.

(b) Meaning discriminations are presented in the source language in both sides of the bidirectional dictionary, as in the fifth edition of Muret-Sander's *Encyclopaedic English-German & German-English dictionary*. And so they are in English in the English-German part, and in German in the German-English part.

(c) Meaning discriminations are presented in the same language in both sides of the bidirectional dictionary, as in M. H. Raventos's *McKay's Modern Spanish-English & English-Spanish Dictionary* where they are presented in English in both parts.

(d) Meaning discriminations are presented in both languages in both sides of the bidirectional dictionary, as in the second edition of J. E. Mansion's *Heath's Standard French & English Dictionary*.

Not only existing dictionaries but also theoreticians disagree on the language in which meaning discriminations are presented. Since Iannucci believes that meaning discrimination is necessary for production only,[57] he recommends that meaning discriminations should be presented in the source language in both sides of the bidirectional dictionary.[58] On the other hand, Williams finds it necessary to provide meaning discriminations in certain cases in both languages, since he believes that meaning discrimination is necessary for both production

---

[57] James E. Ianucci, "Meaning discrimination in bilingual dictionaries," in Householder and Saporta, p. 204.
    [58] *Ibid.*, p. 206.

and (sometimes) comprehension, and that each side of the dictionary serves these two purposes at the same time.[59]

The solution proposed in this book is based on the typology presented in Chapter 2. Taking into consideration that each dictionary should serve one purpose only (either production or comprehension) and one speaker only (either the speaker of the source language or the speaker of the target language) one can well understand that meaning discriminations should be provided in the source language if the dictionary is intended for the speakers of the source language, and in the target language if the dictionary is meant for the speakers of the target language. In other words, meaning discriminations should be presented in the native language of the users for whom the dictionary is prepared.

4.2.5 Because the use of meaning discrimination for every target equivalent is space-consuming and perhaps unsatisfactory, Iannucci proposed that the definitions of the numbered senses in a mono-lingual dictionary should be used as meaning discriminations for the equivalents cited in a bilingual dictionary. And so the translation-equivalents in the bilingual dictionary should have numbers referring to definitions having identical numbers in the monolingual dictionary, or the bilingual dictionary can be run at the bottom of each page of a monolingual dictionary.[60] Iannucci provided the following sample:

Source Dictionary

(19) bolt n. 1. a movable bar which when slid into a socket fastens a door, gate, etc. 2. the part of a lock which is protruded from and drawn back into the case, as by the action of the key. 3. a strong metal pin, often with a head at one end and with a screw thread at the other to receive a nut. See illus. under nut. 4. a sudden swift motion or escape. 5. sudden desertion of a meeting, political party, program, etc. 6. a woven length of cloth. 7. a roll of wall paper. 8. a sudden dash, run, flight, etc. 9. a jet of water, molten glass, etc. 10. an arrow esp. one for a crossbow. 11. a shaft of lightning; a thunderbolt.

Target Dictionary

bolt n. 1 Riegel, 2 Falle, Riegel 3 Bolz 4 Sprung davon 5 Abfall, Abtrünnigkeit 6, 7, Rolle 8 Struz, Flucht 9 Strahl 10 Bolz 11 Blitz-strahl, Donnerkeil.

---

[59] Edwin B. Williams, "Analysis of the problem of meaning discrimination in Spanish and English bilingual lexicography," *Babel*, 6 (1960), p. 123.

[60] James E. Iannucci, "Meaning discrimination in bilingual dictionaries: a new lexicographical technique," *Modern Language Journal*, XLI (1957), p. 278.

A serious objection to Iannucci's proposal is that although it makes the same demands (if not more) on space as those made by the method of complete discrimination, it is cumbersome and impractical. As Hietsch pointed out, the suggested method "puts a heavy strain on the patience of the user, whose eyes are thus expected to travel from one book to another, or at least to the bottom of the page, where incidentally, they are liable to be caught by identical numberings of functional subdivisions (n. : adj., v.t. : v.i., etc.)."[61] Besides, the structural diversity of the vocabulary between any two languages makes it very difficult to use the definitions of a monolingual dictionary as meaning discriminations for the bilingual one.[62]

Referring to the source word by S, the source language discrimination by s, the target word by T, the target language discrimination by t, and polysemy by *, Williams set up the following formulas for meaning discrimination :

$$S = T^*(t)$$ as in example (8)
$$S^* = (s) T; (s) T$$ as in example (9)
$$S^* = (s) T^* (t); (s) T^*(t) ...$$ as in the following example :

(20) race s (contest of speed) carrera (pugna de velocidad); (subdivision of mankind) raza (subdivision del genero human).[63]

In addition to the fact that such entries are confusing and tiring to the user's eyes, they make the dictionary bulky and expensive. As Williams admitted after he had presented his formulas :

> ...there are other questions that need to be answered first that might affect the discrimination of which language the discrimination should be in. The most important of these are (a) the question as to which of the two purposes of the speaker, namely, that involved in working from his own language to the foreign language and that involved in working from the foreign language to his own, is more important per se and more important to a large number of people....[64]

It is clear that the source of Williams' trouble is the multiplicity of purposes, i.e. he wants each side of the bidirectional dictionary to serve two purposes at the same time : production for the speakers of the source language and comprehension for the speakers of the target language. The problems Williams referred to in the quotation

---

[61] Otto Hietsch, "Meaning discrimination in modern lexicography," *Modern Language Journal*, XLII (1958), p. 233.

[62] *Ibid.*

[63] Edwin B. Williams, "Analysis of the problem of meaning discrimination in Spanish and English bilingual lexicography," *Babel*, 6 (1960), p. 124.

[64] *Ibid.*

can be solved to the satisfaction of everybody if the typology presented in Chapter 2 is adopted. The formulas will be simplified as follows :

In a dictionary for production, meaning discrimination should be achieved according to the following formulas :

S* = (s) T; (s) T; ... e.g. suicide s (act) suicidio; (person) suicide.

S* = (st) T*; (st) T*; ... e.g. race s (contest of speed carrera; subdivision of mankind) raza.

And in a dictionary for comprehension, the following two formulas should be adopted :

S = (t) T* e.g. suicidio m (act) suicide

S* = (ts) T*; (ts) T*; ... e.g. carrera f (running place) run; (contest of speed) race.

In these formulas :

S = the source word

s = the source language discrimination presented in the source language.

T = the target word.

t = the target language discrimination presented in the target language.

* = having more than one meaning.

st = meaning discrimination common between the source and target words presented in the source language.

ts = meaning discrimination common between the source and target words presented in the target language.

It should be noted that the formulas proposed here get rid of such cumbersome entries permitted by Williams' formulas as in example (20). They also indicate the language in which meaning discriminations should be presented. The formulas imply that language discriminations are usually placed before the translation equivalents unless there is a particular reason for placing them after the target word as in the case of objects or types of objects which discriminate verbs as in example (16). As pointed out in the formulas, meaning discriminations should be provided systematically and consistently.

4.3 *Word Family Recognition*

4.3.1   In one of his lectures on lexicography, Sledd raised the question : "What attempt can be made in the dictionary to recognize relationships among words?"[65] This question is of paramount importance and although recognized by linguists and lexicographers, little has been done about it in dictionaries. Johnson was well aware of the problem when he said :

> It is of great importance in examining the general fabric of a language, to trace one word from another, by noting the usual modes of derivation and inflection.[66]

Sledd's question has a pedagogical significance as well. Psycholinguistic research has demonstrated that perception of relationships among bits of information facilitates learning and increases retention.

> Whenever intraverbal connections are available, it is as if some of the learning had already occurred before the experiment began. This previous learning is transferred to the new situation. One of the most useful tricks for learning material rapidly is to associate it with something you have already learned.[67]

The bilingual dictionary is expected to pay greater attention to the problem of showing the relationships among related words because of its instructional significance. Unfortunately, aside from bilingual dictionaries dealing with Semitic languages, very few dictionaries have given serious thought to this issue.

4.3.2   In our search for a technique which might enable us to indicate relationships among words belonging to the same family in the dictionary, several alternatives readily present themselves :

(a) Root arrangement of entries :

Since the alphabetical order breaks things into fortuitous pieces, one may think of arranging the dictionary entries according to another order, namely, the root arrangement, where vocabulary is presented in word families. Accordingly the words "like, unlike, dislike, likely, unlikely, likelihood, likeness, likewise, and liking" are all entered in one place under the base word "like." Some linguists think that this is "the only arrangement which can clarify derivational affinities within each root, semantic evolution and etymological relationship."[68] This type of arrangement of entries is very popular in the monolingual dictionaries of the so-called "derivational languages" such as Arabic

---

[65] Professor Sledd's lectures on lexicography at the University of Texas at Austin, Fall semester, 1971.

[66] Samuel Johnson, *Dictionary of the English Language* (London, 1833), p. 3.

[67] George A. Miller, *Language and Communication* (New York : McGraw-Hill, 1963), p. 212.

[68] Regis Blachère *et al. Dictionnaire Arabe-Français-Anglais* (Paris : 1967), p. ix.

and Hebrew. Even the first edition of *Dictionnaire de l'Académie Française*, which appeared in 1694, was based on the root arrangement.

However, the root arrangement has some obvious disadvantages. First, it requires a considerable grammatical sophistication on the part of the dictionary user. Should we expect the layman to guess that the foreign word "acknowledgement" is listed under "know?" Secondly, even if the dictionary user was able to deduce the required root, he would still have to read right through the article to find the word he was looking up. It is obvious, then, that such an arrangement is avoided for practical reasons. And this is what Mary Haas meant when she defined the good dictionary as "one in which you can find what you are looking for—preferably on the first try."[69]

Some lexicographers tried a combination of both arrangements. In his *Diccionario Critico Etimologico de la Langua Castellana*, Corminas lists at the end of the article of the key word, all related words with reduced or no information. He also lists these related words in their proper alphabetical position with a cross reference to the key word. Although this procedure is somewhat economical for his purpose, Hall criticized it because "the number of cross references causes a great deal of page-turning, often to distant parts of the work, ..."[70] Thus superfluous opportunities for the user to deepen his understanding of the morphological structure of the word and of its semantic relations to other words derived from the same root also make the dictionary difficult to use. A lexicographer should do his best to spare the learner of the foreign language from any unnecessary difficulty.

(b) Morphological rewriting:

Another technique for recognizing relationships among derivatives was proposed by Hill about a quarter of a century ago. He recommended that the article of the dictionary entry should include morphological rewriting (similar to the pronunciation rewriting) which can be achieved by using hyphens, points, or similar notations to mark morpheme boundaries. Thus the entry "unlikely" should be followed by a morphological rewriting: (un/like/ly). Such a morphological analysis would assist the dictionary user in perceiving the relationship between the word he is looking up and the other related words he has

---

[69] Mary R. Haas, "What belongs in a bilingual dictionary?" in Householder and Saporta, p. 48.

[70] Robert A. Hall, Jr. "Review of Diccionario critico etimologico de la langua castellana, by J. Corminas," *Language*, 39 (1963), p. 116.

already learned, and consequently the learning load would be reduced.[71] This idea was reintroduced by other linguists concerned with lexicography such as Kemp Malone and Richard Harrel at the Indiana University Conference on Lexicography in 1960.

Hill's proposal runs into two difficulties : first, its application to commercial lexicography presupposes clear-cut boundaries between morphemes. Unfortunately morphologists have not yet reached an overall agreement on these boundaries. Second, this method might work when applied to derived words whose morphemes are distinct like "mankind," but it is not feasible in the case of derived words whose morphemes are not so obvious like "monetary" and "men," nor is it helpful in the case of simple words like "man." Here the dictionary user's attention cannot be attracted to the related words such as "manly, manhood, mannish, manlike, mankind, chairman, gentleman, layman, etc."

(c) Truncated definitions as a means of word family recognition :

A third approach to the problem of the recognition of the relationships among words in the dictionary is proposed by Gove. His suggestion can be termed the "truncated definitions" technique. Truncated definitions are those "which employ a formula involving a base word or a homograph by functional shift..."[72] Accordingly, truncated definitions include four kinds :

(i) Definitions which employ the base word of the form defined, as in *broadly* adv. : in a broad manner.

(ii) Definitions of a transitive verb which include its intransitive cognate, or vice versa, as in *change* vi : to change one's clothes.

(iii) The verb definition which contains one of the participle forms of that verb as in *snore* vt : to spend (time) in snoring, and *impregnate* vi : to become impregnated.

(iv) The definitions of one of the numbered senses which uses a preceding sense, as in peach n :

   (1) tree
   (2) the edible fruit of the peach.[73]

Gove argues that truncated definitions should be used freely to relate

---

[71] Archibald A. Hill, "The use of dictionaries in language teaching," *Language Learning*, 1 (1948), p. 10.

[72] Philip B. Gove, "Repetition in defining," *College Composition and Communication* (1965). Reprinted in Philip B. Gove (ed.) *The Role of the Dictionary* (Indianapolis : The Bobbs-Merrill Co., Inc., 1967), p. 9.

[73] *Ibid.*, p. 11.

words to each other in families, and this will result in a considerable facility in using the words :

> The truncated analytic definition may be used freely, and should be used in the definition of family words and cognates wherever brevity is attained without the sacrifice of clarity and without objectional circularity.[74]

To cite an example from *Webster's Seventh New Collegiate Dictionary*, the *prank* family presents no problem :

> prank n : TRICK
> prankish adj 1 : full of pranks 2 : having the nature of prank.
> prankishly adv : (an undefined run-on)
> prankishness n : (an undefined run-on)
> prankster n : a player of pranks.

But the above-mentioned example is oversimplified and numbers of word families are not usually so simply arranged or neatly related. Besides, the use of truncated definitions in the dictionary should be restricted in the following ways.

(1) Circularity should be avoided. If the definition of A uses B, then the definition of B should not use A. Circularity can be avoided if the base word is given a primary definition. For example, the word beauty (n.) should be adequately defined first, then the words "beauteous, beautiful, beautify, and beautification" may use the base word *beauty* in their definitions.[75]

(2) The truncated definition of a family word should move in the direction of the base word and not away from it.

(3) The dictionary user should not be put through more than one rerouting within the family before he is presented with the primary definition.

(4) The truncated definition should be modified when the defined word extends beyond the meaning of the base word, as in *builder* n : "one who builds or oversees building operations."

(5) The truncated definition should include particularization or a specification when the base word has several numbered senses.[76]

Three serious objections can be made to this technique : first, it is difficult to abide by the rules for the adequate use of truncated definitions. Even *Webster's Seventh New Collegiate Dictionary* (*WSNC*), which was edited by Gove himself, violates these rules which were emphasized by its editor-in-chief. The following are examples of its violations :

---

[74] *Ibid.*
[75] *Ibid.*
[76] *Ibid.*, pp. 11-13.

(1) Several of its truncated definitions put the dictionary user through more than one rerouting before he arrives at the primary definition. To cite one of numerous examples let us look up the adjective *perfectible* :

>perfectible adj...capable of improvement or perfection.

So we should look up the word *perfection* :

>perfection n 1 ...the quality or state of being perfect.

And now we have to look up the word *perfect*, which is listed above *perfectible* and which is given the primary definition. The lexicographer can avoid putting the user through more than one rerouting within the family by rewording the definition of *perfectible* to read "capable of becoming, or being made, perfect" and *perfect* should be given the primary· definition.

(2) Several truncated definitions in *WSNC* refer the dictionary user to a base word which involves several numbered senses and subsenses. But those truncated definitions do not include any particularization or specification which might assist the user in selecting the related sense. The verb *mature* may serve as an example :

>mature vt : to bring to maturity or completion.
>maturity n 1 : the quality or state of being mature.
>mature adj 1... 2a(1)... 2a(2)... 2b... etc.

Looking up the same verb in the *American College Dictionary*,[77] we notice that the editor did not only reduce the number of the annoying reroutings, but his truncated definition includes the desired specification :

>mature : vt : to make mature esp. to ripen,

(3) Several of *WSNC*'s truncated definitions use critical base words which are not included in the dictionary at all. A flagrant example is the word *Muhammadan* :

>Muhammadan adj : of or relating to Muhammad or Islam—Muhammadan n—Muhammadanism.

Here the meanings of the main entry and its two run-ons depend on the base word *Muhammad*. If you try to look up this base word in the dictionary, you will never find it. The reason is obvious, namely that *WSNC* excludes all proper names.

The writer of this book is of the opinion that when the editor adopts the policy of excluding encyclopedic materials from his dictionary,

---

[77] C. L. Barnhart, ed. *The American College Dictionary* (New York : Random House, 1966).

those proper names whose derivations are entered should be retained for the sake of clarity and the recognition of the relationships among words of the same family.

The second objection pertains to the treatment of idioms. It goes without saying that a word family does not include the single lexical item derived from the base word only, but extends to all idioms that contain the base word or one of its derivatives. Since the idiom has "a meaning that cannot be derived from the conjoined meanings of its elements,"[78] Gove's truncated definition will not help here. The definition of the idiom does not show the relationship between that idiom and the other members of word family; for example:

> Kick the bucket *slang*: DIE

Even if truncated definitions could be employed in defining idioms, they would be able to show only the relationship between the idiom and its base words, but not the relationships among the other members of the word family.

Another reason why the relationship between idioms and their base words is lost is the arrangement which some dictionaries (including *WSNC*) adopts in listing idioms. Idioms which are made up of V + NP (kick the bucket), V + Pre + NP (kick over the traces), or V + adv (kick upstairs) are treated within the article of the main entry. Whereas idioms which consist of V + adv. particle (kick in) are entered separately. *WSNC*'s entries, for instance, are arranged in strict "alphabetical order letter by letter. For example *book of account* follows *bookmobile* as if it were printed *bookofaccount* with no space in the middle."[79] As a result of this type of extreme alphabetical arrangement, idioms do not follow their base words; and thus we find *pick off* following *pickle*, *send away* following *sandal*, and *put away* following *putative*.

One of the solutions to this organizational problem is to list all the related idioms below the base word, not within its article, but in main entries. This procedure is followed, for example, in the *American College Dictionary*.

The last and most important objection—as far as this book is concerned—to the technique of truncated definition is that it does not work in bilingual dictionaries where entry words are usually not defined but given translation-equivalents.

---

[78] From the definition of the word *idiom* in *WSNC*.
[79] Philip B. Gove, ed. *Webster's Third New International Dictionary*, p. 6.

4.3.3   Having examined the various theoretical and practical methods of indicating relationships among words in the dictionary, and having pointed out their shortcomings and limitations, this writer here proposes a new approach which is theoretically sound and practically feasible. The dictionary should provide a word family study wherever appropriate. The quantity of this proposed study depends on the space available. Generally speaking, entries should include between brackets all or the most frequent derivatives of the base word.

For example :

Comfort   (comfortable, uncomfortable, comforter, comforting, comfortless).

Much space can be saved if lexicographical conventions are used; e.g. :

comfort (-able, un-able, -er, -ing, -less)

A derivative might be followed by the base word and some other closely related words of its family; e.g. :

uncomfortable (comfort, comfortable)

These words between brackets may serve as hints to remind the foreign language learner of other related words he might have previously learned and so facilitate learning.

As for idioms, they should be listed in separate entries immediately after the base words. In some dictionaries, like *Larousse Modern Dictionary*,[80] idioms are also listed in boldface letters in a box exactly under the main entry; e.g. :

break v :

1.   to break away— 2.   to break down— 3.   to break in— 4.   to break off— 5.   to break through— 6.   to break up...

The proposed technique, i.e. listing the members of the word family after each entry, shows at a glance which are the words related to that particular entry, and consequently results in easier learning and greater retention.

---

[80] Marguerite-Marie Dubois, ed. *Larousse French-English & English-French Modern Dictionary* (Paris : Larousse, 1969).

CHAPTER FIVE

OTHER RELATED PROBLEMS

5.1 *Usage*

5.1.1 Usage can be defined as the study of socially graded synonyms. "Ain't I" and "am I not," for instance, have the same meaning, but quite different social values. The way you talk tells people who you are and who you would like to be. Slang, for example, is the language of the rebels who do not use the language of the establishment. The moment that respectable people use slang, it is no longer used by the rebels; its social status changes and it is no longer considered slang.[1] Usage is not limited to vocabulary only but covers spelling (alright vs. all right), pronunciation (cents), and grammar (ain't I).

As for recording usage in dictionaries, there are two traditions in English : (a) prescriptive, and (b) descriptive.

(a) Prescriptive dictionaries label usage with a censorious tone. This tradition was established in English by Samuel Johnson who stated in the introduction to his dictionary that "every language has likewise its improprieties and absurdities, which it is the duty of the lexicographer to correct or proscribe."[2] To Dr. Johnson, the function of the dictionary was one "by which the pronunciation of our language may be fixed and its attainment facilitated; by which its purity may be preserved, its use ascertained, and its duration lengthened."[3] Accordingly, Johnson labeled *excepting*, for example, as "an improper word," and condemned such items as *budge*, *fun*, and *clever* with the label "a low word." Johnson's prescriptive tendencies had their origins in European lexicography and in the English philosophy of grammar. The Académie Française, which was founded in 1635, assumed the role of an authority in the French linguistic and literary world, and prepared a dictionary aiming at the regulation of the French tongue. In seventeenth-and-eighteenth-century England, grammarians assumed that their task was to perfect the language by giving it logical rules.

---

[1] James Sledd, lectures on Lexicography at the University of Texas, Fall 1971.

[2] Samuel Johnson, *A Dictionary of the English Language* (London : T. T. and J. Tegg *et al.*, 1833), p. 1.

[3] *Ibid.*

Aikin stated in the preface to his *The English Grammar* that a grammar "ought to be the standard of the English Tongue..."[4]

(b) Descriptive dictionaries try to be objective recorders of the language and tend to use a semantically neutral terminology in describing usage. The descriptive tradition was established by the *Oxford English Dictionary* which states the function of the dictionary as follows :

> The aim of this dictionary is to present in alphabetical series the words which have formed the English vocabulary from the time of the earliest records down to the present day, with all the relevant facts concerning their form, sense, history, pronunciation and etymology. It embraces not only the standard language of literature and conversation, whether current at the moment or obsolete, or archaic, but also the main technical vocabulary, and a large measure of dialectal usage and slang.[5]

This tradition has been growing in American lexicography since the turn of the century. Dr. Funk wrote in the preface of his 1913 *Standard Dictionary of the English Language* saying that "the chief function of a dictionary is to record usage." But he added that a dictionary should "give its sanction to the best forms and tendencies."[6] The 1934 *Webster's New International Dictionary* rejected the prescriptive tradition for it aimed at recording the "best present usage." The 1961 *Webster's Third* wholly accepted the descriptive trend [7] by recording "general cultivated conversational usage, both formal and informal."[8] Another feature of the descriptive trend in *Webster's Third* was summed up by Gove, its editor-in-chief, in a letter he sent to the editor of Life Magazine in which he said :

> The responsibility of a dictionary is to record the language, not set its style. For us to attempt to prescribe the language would be like *Life* reporting the news as its editors would prefer it to happen.[9]

5.1.2 Modern linguists differentiate between correctness and style. Correctness cannot be established by an authority, whether an indi-

---

[4] Joseph Aikin, *The English Grammar* (London, 1693), as quoted in *Working With Aspects of Language*, by Mansoor Alyeshmerni and Paul Tauber (New York : Harcourt, Brace & World, Inc., 1970), p. 227.

[5] James Murray *et al.* eds., *The Oxford English Dictionary* (Oxford : The Clarendon Press, 1933), p. v.

[6] Isaac K. Funk, *New Standard Dictionary* (New York : Funk & Wagnalls, 1913), p. vi.

[7] Albert H. Marckwardt, "Dictionaries and the English language," *The English Journal*, 52 (1963), p. 339.

[8] Gove, *Webster's Third New International Dictionary*, p. 6a.

[9] From a letter by Philip B. Gove to the editor of *Life Magazine*, published in *Life*, Nov. 17, 1961, p. 13. Reprinted in Sledd and Ebbitt, p. 22.

vidual or a book, nor by appealing to logic, analogy or the historical development of the language. Instead, correctness should be based on actual usage of educated speakers of the language.[10] "Any form," said Hill, "is correct if it is current in the dialect... that the writer is using."[11] Incorrectness can result from the use of the forms of a dialect in an inappropriate situation. In the words of Hill :

> ...it is as serious an error to use the forms of Standard English where they are socially out of place as it is to use Gullah in the pages of a learned article. Incorrectness can result also ... from the mixture of dialects or the improper imitation of a dialect.[12]

But does that mean that the dictionary should record all the forms equally without any comment? Or should it furnish the guidance for style?

The present writer believes that a dictionary should be fully descriptive. It should record objectively various dialects and different styles (unless its purpose is limited to one dialect or one style) as well as inform the user about the attitude of the society or certain sectors of it towards particular linguistic forms.[13] This type of information is very valuable in a bilingual dictionary. The learner of the foreign language wants to know whether a particular linguistic form is formal or informal, and on what occasions he can use it. The dictionary should indicate whether a form, for example, can be used when children are present, adults of one sex only, or when the group is mixed. It should also indicate whether or not a form is formal, appropriate in a religious place or a public meeting. As DeCamp rightly puts it :

> ...he [the student] must know *when* he should use it [the linguistic construction]. This includes understanding the meaning and also the social implications of a statement. Is it casual and slangy, suitable only for use among personal friends of equal status, like the American greeting *Hi!*, or is it courteous and formal, suitable for use in situations requiring respect?[14]

---

[10] Thomas Pyles, "Dictionaries and usage," in *Linguistics Today* ed. by Archibald A. Hill (New York : Basic Books, Inc., 1969), pp. 132-133.

[11] Archibald A. Hill, "Correctness and style in English composition," in *A Linguistic Reader*, ed. by Graham Wilson (New York : Harper & Row, 1967), p. 50.

[12] *Ibid.*, p. 51.

[13] William Morris, ed. *The American Heritage Dictionary* (Boston : American Heritage Publishing Co., 1969), p. vi.

[14] David DeCamp, "Linguistics and teaching foreign language," in *Linguistics Today*, ed. by Archibald A. Hill, p. 147.

However, there are two major issues which the lexicographer should attend to before he uses these restrictive or usage labels : (5.1.3) how to record usage, and (5.1.4) what labels to use.

5.1.3   Since modern linguists decided that there is no single standard or "correctness" in usage and that the etymology of a word has no relevance for its present meaning or usage,[15] the lexicographer is faced with the problem of selecting the proper means for describing usage. As Gove worded the question :

> Let us instead of arguing about such labels as *colloq*, *informal*, *vulgar*, *low*, and *slang* settle for the use of a sign—an obelus ($\div$)—to mean 'people have divided opinions about the propriety of this word' or 'some people consider this inelegant.' Who will take the responsibility for scattering the sign throughout the dictionary? What will it mean to the user?[16]

Two methods have been already suggested by American lexicographers to record levels of usage as accurately as possible :

(a) Barnhart proposed the use of questionnaires for help in framing the qualifying or restrictive labels as well as in applying these labels to linguistic forms. The opinions should be collected, analyzed, and reviewed by an editorial advisory committee, and a final decision should be made by the editor.[17]

(b) Another way of getting information about usage is called the "usage panel" or "jury" method which was employed in the making of the *American Heritage Dictionary*. A hundred outstanding speakers and writers were chosen and asked a wide range of questions about controversial usage. Their replies were tabulated and analyzed, and the editors prepared usage notes which said, for example, 90% of the panel accepted this linguistic form in writing.[18] Many objections were made to this method. Although Hill accepted the establishment of such a panel in principle, he made specific criticisms of how the panel was chosen and how it was used. The panel was not a "random sampling of a larger population" and it was not used consistently or systematically.[19] Read objects completely to the use of the jury method for

---

[15] Robert A. Hall, Jr., "Telling the truth," *The Quarterly Journal of Speech*, 48 (1962), p. 57.

[16] Philip B. Gove, "Usage in the dictionary," in *The Role of the Dictionary*, ed. by Philip B. Gove (Indianapolis : Bobbs-Merrill Co., 1967), p. 57.

[17] C. L. Barnhart, "Problems in editing commercial monolingual dictionaries," in Householder and Saporta, pp. 178-180.

[18] William Morris, *The American Heritage Dictionary*, p. vii.

[19] Archibald A. Hill, "Laymen, lexicographers, and linguists," *Language*, 46 (1970), pp. 246-247.

usage because "sentences *about* usage are of an utterly different order from the sentences that exemplify usage."[20]

5.1.4 The second major problem pertaining to the use of usage labels in the dictionary is the denotations of these labels. Labels mean different things to different lexicographers and different users. People do not come to an agreement about usage labels such as "colloquial," "slang," and "popular." "Colloquial," as Gove pointed out, "has been almost universally misunderstood and misused..."[21] and so it is sometimes confused with "localism" and sometimes taken to mean "low word." Fries made a similar comment on the label "slang :"

> The term 'slang' has suffered such a wide extension of its signification and has been applied to so many varieties of words that it is extremely difficult to draw the line between what is slang and what is not.[22]

In order to see whether American lexicographers have similar understandings of the signification of the usage labels they employ in their dictionaries, the present writer looked up several items in five major American dictionaries : *The American Heritage Dictionary* (AHD), *The American College Dictionary* (ACD), *Webster's New International Dictionary, Second Edition* (W2), the *Random House Dictionary* (RHD), and *Funk and Wagnall's New "Standard" Dictionary* (F&W). The results which are summarized in Table 1 demonstrate that there is no con-

Table 1

	ACD	AHD	F & W	RHD	W2
ain't	illiterate or dialectical	nonstandard	Colloq.	Nonstandard in U.S. except in some dialects, informal in Britain	Dialectical or illiterate
boss	chiefly U.S. Colloq.	—	Colloq. U.S.	—	Colloq.
goof	Slang	Slang	(not listed)	Slang	Slang U.S.
monkey	Colloq.	informal	—		
movie	U.S. Colloq.	informal	Colloq. U.S.	informal	Slang U.S.
piffle	Colloq.	—	Slang	informal	Slang
pig	Colloq.	informal	—	informal	Slang

---

[20] Allen Walker Read, "Approaches to lexicography and semantics," in *Modern Trends in Linguistics 10*, ed. by Thomas Sebeok (The Hague : Mouton, 1972), p. 606.

[21] Philip B. Gove, "Usage in the dictionary," in *The Role of the Dictionary*, ed. by Gove (Indianapolis : Bobbs-Merrill Co., 1967), p. 52.

[22] Charles C. Fries, "Usage levels and dialect distribution," in *The American College Dictionary*, ed. by C. L. Barnhart, p. xxv.

sistency in labeling words; the same word used in the same way might
be labeled differently in different dictionaries.

5.1.5   The present writer thinks that the common and traditional view,
i.e. words are either correct or incorrect and lexicographers should
employ usage labels to indicate these common errors is not supported
by modern linguistics. But he also thinks that a bilingual dictionary
should be fully descriptive and furnish guidance in style as well as
attitudes of the language community towards particular linguistic
forms. Accordingly the bilingual dictionary should employ two types
of usage labels : (a) linguistic labels such as standard, nonstandard,
local, and poetic, and (b) social labels such as friendly use, offensive,
derogatory, hostile, and contemptuous. Unless the dictionary provides
these linguistic and social types of information on usage, the foreign
user of the dictionary might produce sentences like "Ladies and
gentlemen: Professor Jones ain't gonna deliver his lecture today,"
and "Luther King was a great nigger."

The best way to get information about usage is not by asking the
outstanding professional speakers and writers of the language to pass
value judgments distinguishing "good" usage from "bad" usage, as
Bishop emphasized,[23] but by carefully observing what kind of people
use the linguistic form and what they actually do when they use it in
speech or writing, and by examining the status of the linguistic form
which is constantly changing.

The signification of each usage label employed in the bilingual
dictionary must be precisely defined in the front matter.

5.2   *Illustrative Examples*

5.2.1   An illustrative example is any phrase or sentence that illustrates
the use of the item defined or translated. "Illustrative examples" is
one of several terms used interchangeably by various writers. The
most widespread of these terms are "contextual examples," "verbal
illustrations," "citations," and "quotations." The last two terms might
be limited to those illustrative examples which are found in actual
speech or writing.

---

[23] Morris Bishop, "Good usage, bad usage, and usage," in *The American Heritage
Dictionary*, p. xxiii.

A distinction should be made between two types of citations:
(a) those examples of usage which are collected and analyzed by the
editor and his assistants for the basis of their definitions or translations,
and (b) those examples which appear in the articles of the dictionary
to illustrate the usage of the entry. However, there is always a definite
relation between the two types. The illustrative examples cited in the
dictionary usually represent a selected sample drawn from the citations
accumulated in the lexicographer's catalogues. This section is chiefly
concerned with those examples that actually appear in the dictionary.

5.2.2   Illustrative examples were first introduced into English lexicography by Johnson in his dictionary which appeared in 1755. According
to Sledd and Kolb, this was Johnson's only innovation as far as
English lexicography was concerned.[24] However, illustrative examples
had been employed in dictionaries a long time before that. They had
been used with various degrees of skill and abundance by the Arab
lexicographers since the eighth century. Even the pioneers of Arabic
lexicography cited numerous quotations from prose and poetry for
each entry.[25] Illustrative examples had been also used by Greek and
Latin lexicographers since the sixteenth century, by the Accademia
della Crusca for Italian, by Bluteau for Portuguese, and by Richelet for
French. In the eighteenth century the Accademia della Crusca took
great care in the choice of the illustrative quotations to provide "a fuller
record of sage ancient and modern, in prose and in poetry, in manuscript
and in print."[26]

5.2.3   Illustrative examples in the dictionary may serve one or more
of the following functions:

(a) They may be used in the dictionary to prove that a word or
a particular meaning of a word exists in the language. The early Arab
lexicographers provided quotations from prose and poetry as evidence
that the word under discussion was found in the Arabic language,
not to illustrate its meaning. That is why those quotations were often
explained and commented on. One reason behind that policy is that
the pioneers of Arabic lexicography aimed at registering the complete

---

[24] James Sledd and Gwin Kolb, *Dr. Johnson's Dictionary* (Chicago: The Univ. of
Chicago Press, 1955), pp. 41-43.

[25] Abdul Karim Germanus, "Studies in Arabic lexicography," *Islamic Quarterly*, 1
(1954), pp. 23-25.

[26] James Sledd and Gwin Kolb, *op. cit.*, p. 42.

lexicon of the language, and so they had to prove the existence of the numerous rare words listed in their dictionaries.[27]

(b) For Johnson, illustrative examples were a sort of defining device; i.e. they served to illustrate the meaning of the word defined, and not merely to prove that the word existed in the language. As he pointed out in his preface :

> It is not sufficient that a word is found, unless it be so combined that its meaning is apparently determined by the tract and tenour of the sentence; ...[28]

Nida, who rejects the definition of meaning as "a common denominator" or "what is common to all situations in which a term is employed," asserts that "the only way to 'define' the meaning of *charge* [for instance] is to describe (usually by illustrative phrases or sentences) the distribution of the word,"[29] and so in order to convey the total meaning of *charge* he cites the following illustrative phrases :

> Charge into the line of players, charge the gun, charge the battery, charge the pencil, charge the man ten dollars, charge the culprit with the crime, he gets a charge out of it, a charge of electricity, he is in charge, he is a public charge.[30]

In other words, contextual examples can serve to illustrate the semantic range or distribution of the word.

Many theoreticians point out that illustrative examples should not take the place of semantic analysis. The lexicographer should not ask the user to analyze the illustrative examples and learn from them things which are not stated explicitly in the dictionary. If the user, for instance, is not told whether the verb can take both animate and inanimate objects, then he can look at the illustrative examples to find out. To depend on quotations in this fashion, as Sledd noted, is cheating on the part of the lexicographer who stops short of doing the descriptive work he ought to do.[31]

(c) Hill would employ contextual examples to illustrate the grammatical (phonological, morphological, syntactic) behavior of the word

---

[27] John A. Haywood, *Arabic Lexicography* (Leiden : Brill, 1960), p. 2.

[28] Samuel Johnson, *A Dictionary of the English Language* (London, 1833), p. 8.

[29] Eugene A. Nida, "Analysis of meaning and dictionary making," International Journal of American Linguistics, 24 (1958), p. 282.

[30] *Ibid.*

[31] James Sledd's lectures on Lexicography at The University of Texas at Austin, Fall 1971.

defined in addition to their illustration of meaning. One of the examples he cited in his model entry on *furniture* is :

We bought three pieces of furniture—a table and two chairs
   2   3   1   2   31
[wibɔ́t θríy piysəzə fɔ́rnɪtšər $\#$ ə téybələn túw tšɛ́rz $\#$][32]

In addition to the fact that this example shows that tables and chairs are items of furniture, it illustrates one of the characteristics of the uncountable, namely the use of an itemizer (piece), and it shows the pronunciation of the word before a double cross, $\#$. The rest of the examples illustrate the other characteristics of the uncountable and the pronunciations of the word in various positions. It should be noted that Hill does not intend to substitute the contextual example for grammatical analysis and statement; he has already labeled the entry word "uncountable" and the grammatical characteristics of this subclass should be stated explicitly in the front matter.

(d) For Gleason, the major function of illustrative examples is to "indicate—largely by the other words in them—something of the stylistic value of the entry."[33] Since a fully descriptive dictionary should provide information on the stylistic implications of its entry words, and since these implications are difficult to define precisely for every word, Gleason believes that a more feasible method is to use carefully chosen illustrative citations.[34]

For the present writer, the primary function of the illustrative examples in dictionaries in general and bilingual ones in particular is to contribute to the user's interest by showing the word in a live context, and to enhance his understanding of the grammatical and semantic rules governing the usage of the word by showing these rules in action. Illustrative examples should not be intended to take the place of grammatical or semantic statements, but they should illustrate them only. In other words, illustrative examples are just examples, a pedagogical device and no more. However abundant these illustrative examples may be, or skilfully employed, "they certainly do not amount to a descriptive statement in the sense of an economical and explicit formulation of distinctive facts."[35]

---

[32] Archibald A. Hill, "Notes on dictionary entries on furniture," mimeographed notes, The University of Texas at Austin, 1971, p. 2.

[33] H. A. Gleason, Jr., *Linguistics and English Grammar* (New York : Holt, Rinehart and Winston, Inc., 1965), p. 429.

[34] *Ibid.*

[35] Uriel Weinreich, "Webster's Third : a critique of its semantics," *International Journal of American Linguistics*, 30 (1964), p. 407.

However, as far as bilingual dictionaries are concerned, the writer suggests that illustrative examples can have an independent function. They can be selected purposefully to give the dictionary user some notions of the foreign culture he is dealing with. The culture can be illustrated, to a great extent, by the quotations cited in the bilingual dictionary.

5.2.4   The selection and presentation of the illustrative examples raise a number of controversial questions, the most important of which are :

(a) Should illustrative examples be coined or rather drawn from actual writing or speech?

The general trend indicates that illustrative citations should have actually been used in writing or speech.[36] However, Hill does not object to coining illustrative examples in a dictionary intended for the foreign learners of the language. Fabricated examples in this case have two advantages : first, they can be tailored to serve their major functions of illustrating the grammatical and semantic usage of the word, and secondly they can be made briefer than the actual quotations and easier to understand.[37]

(b) From which period of the language should the illustrative examples be drawn?

Three distinct schools of thought can be found :

(i) The first maintains that citations should be drawn from "the golden age" of the language when the language was still "pure" because the speakers had not yet intermixed with foreign elements, and their speech had not been spoiled by translating from foreign languages. The early Arab lexicographers limited their quotations to the literature of the pre-Islamic and Early Islamic periods, or specifically to pre-Islamic poetry, the Quran, and the Hadith (Oral Tradition).[38] Johnson's "golden age" for English was from the time of Sidney to the Restoration and accordingly he drew his citations from the writers of that period.[39]

(ii) The second maintains that the citations of a descriptive dictionary should be drawn mostly from contemporary writers regardless of their lasting literary quality. In the words of Marckwardt :

---

[36] Philip B. Gove, ed. *Webster's Third New International Dictionary*, p. 6a.

[37] Professor Hill's views as expressed to the writer in person.

[38] Ibrahim Madkur, *Fi 'l-lughati wa 'l-adab* (Cairo: Dāru 'l-Maʿārif, 1971), p. 109.

[39] James Sledd, lectures on Lexicography at The University of Texas at Austin, Fall 1971.

...the overriding concern of the dictionary is quite appropriately the language in its current state. It is on these grounds that the editors may logically justify the preponderance of citations from current authors, irrespective of lasting literary merit.[40]

This school of thought rejects the notion that not many contemporary authors deserve quotation because "it is only another form of the notion that the lexicographer should be a law-giver and not a historian."[41] However, some practical considerations may determine the question of lasting literary merit. If the dictionary is scheduled to be revised periodically, as in the case of *Webster's International Dictionary*, which is scheduled to be revised almost every 25 years, then the requirement of lasting literary merit can be overlooked since many of the quotations will be discarded in the new edition. But if there is no plan for a new edition of the dictionary, then the editor should perhaps try to draw his quotations from outstanding authors of lasting reputation, as is done in the *Oxford English Dictionary*.[42]

(iii) The third maintains that citations should be drawn from all the periods of the language in order to produce a well-balanced book. The dictionary should not emphasize the present at the expense of the past nor the past at the expense of the present.[43] Barnhart noted that from a practical point of view, a commercial dictionary should include "words in actual use in the literature (reading matter) of today and the literature of the past that is widely read and studied today."[44] Another advantage claimed for well-balanced citations is that they can show the age of the word and the changes in spelling it underwent especially when the earliest and the latest occurrences are cited.[45]

(c) Should the authors and sources of the illustrative examples be identified?

Let us consider the following example :

¹ Chase...vb...4a : to cause to depart or flee esp. by the use of or threat of violence or other harassment : DRIVE, EXPEL, DISPEL love hath

---

[40] Albert H. Marckwardt, "Dictionaries and the English language," p. 341.

[41] James Sledd, "The lexicographer's uneasy chair," in *Dictionaries and That Dictionary*, ed. by Sledd and Ebbitt, p. 231.

[42] Marckwardt, *op. cit.*

[43] Dwight MacDonald, "Three questions for structural linguists on Webster 3 revisited," in *Dictionaries and That Dictionary*, ed. by Sledd and Ebbitt, p. 256.

[44] C. L. Barnhart, "Problems in editing commercial monolingual dictionaries," in Householder and Saporta, p. 161.

[45] James A. H. Murray *et al. The Oxford English Dictionary* (Oxford : The Clarendon Press, 1933), p. xxii.

chased sleep from my enthralled eyes—Shak. I'll~the whole rebel army all the way to South Carolina—Kenneth Roberts.~cattle out of a wheat field...[46]

In the above-cited entry, the first two illustrative citations are identified as to the author only, but not the source (i.e. the title of the book, the edition and the number of the page). The third is an unidentified citation. There are two points of view regarding the identification of citations :

(i) Quotations should be fully identified to make it possible to check and examine them in their contexts to see whether their original meaning was misrepresented because of abridgement or other causes.[47]

(ii) It is not necessary to identify the quotation because it is not important who used the word, but how it was used. Besides, "precise references would take up much valuable space."[48]

(d) Should authors be quoted for their use of words only or for their opinions also?

The general trend is that "authors are quoted for their use of words or for the structural pattern of their words but not for their opinions or sentiment,"[49] because "a dictionary," as Gelb thinks of it, "is not a world of ideas but a repository of words."[50] But, as already stated, illustrative examples can be so selected or made up as to reflect the culture and the patterns of thinking and social behavior of the speakers of the target language. By so doing, citations can become more informative and more interesting.

(e) Should the presentation of the several citations illustrating one word follow a certain order?

Before the nineteenth century the presentation of quotations did not follow any particular order. In 1812, Passow laid down the principles of the chronological arrangement of citations in his Greek dictionary.[51] In the *Oxford English Dictionary*, a citation is given for each century in order to show the history of the word and its development.

---

[46] *Webster's Third New International Dictionary*.

[47] Murray *et al. Op. cit.*, p. xxxii.

[48] James Sledd, "The lexicographer's uneasy chair," p. 231.

[49] Philip B. Gove, *Webster's Third New International Dictionary*, p. 6a.

[50] I. J. Gelb, "Lexicography, lexicology, and the Accadian dictionary," in *"A André Martinet" « E structuralismo e Historia »* Vol. II (Canarias : Universidad de la Laguna, 1958), p. 73.

[51] *Ibid.*, p. 72.

(f) How much space should be devoted to illustrative examples?

According to Barnhart, college dictionaries devote from .7 to 1.3 per cent of their space to illustrative examples and from 54 to 61 per cent to definitions. In commercial dictionaries, the use of illustrative examples is incidental and inconsistent. An example is the number of citations in *Al-Mawrid: A Modern English-Arabic Dictionary*. Although it is stated in its introduction that "the great majority" of the words are used in contextual sentences or phrases,[52] a simple statistical study conducted by the writer showed that only a minority of senses (about 14.76%) are illustrated by citations.[53]

5.2.5 The purpose of the dictionary should be to act as a guide in solving the problems raised in (5.2.4). If the dictionary is historical, then the quotations should be drawn from the period or periods which the dictionary treats, and they should be presented in a chronological order. In a bilingual dictionary, it is preferable to give citations which have been actually used in writing or speech, but if brief and appropriate citations are not available, the lexicographer and his assistants may make up their own provided that they are native speakers of the language or are using native informants. Full identification of quotations is not necessary in the bilingual dictionary because it is space-consuming and the user does not normally need it. But attributing the illustrative example to its author might contribute considerably to the user's interest, especially if the author was well-known to him.

Aside from these borderline cases, there are four principles which should govern the use of illustrative examples in the bilingual dictionary:

---

[52] Munir Ba'alabaki, *Al-Mawrid: A Modern English-Arabic Dictionary* (Beirut: Dar El-Ilm Lil-Malayēn, 1967), p. ii.

[53] Three pages were picked randomly; their main entries, the separate senses of each entry, and the illustrative phrases and sentences were counted. This procedure was repeated twice with other pages; the results were verified. The first three pages were:

Page numbers	Contents of each page		
	main entries	separate senses	illustrative examples
268	56	98	20
673	45	84	14
988	57	109	9
Total:	158	291	43

(1) The illustrative examples should be used systematically and consistently. Each separate meaning of every entry should be illustrated by one citation at least.

(2) The illustrative examples should be translated into the user's native language. Otherwise they will become useless or time-consuming because they very probably will contain some other words whose meaning is unknown to the user.

(3) The illustrative examples should be so selected as to reflect the culture of the speakers of the target language.

(4) The illustrative examples should be brief and informative. They should really illustrate the use of the word and enhance the user's understanding of its grammatical behavior, semantic range, stylistic affiliations, or all of these.

5.3 *Pictorial Illustrations*

5.3.1 The term "pictorial illustrations," as used in this book, takes Fleming's definition as a point of departure. Fleming defined pictorial illustrations as "those configurations of line, dot, or area and any combination of these three resembling events or objects (persons, places, and/or things) either as perceived or as generally conceived."[54] The definition should be expanded to include such borderline cases as number lines, geometric figures, structural chemical formulas, curves, graphs, and time lines. A pictorial illustration in a dictionary should also be expanded to include the verbal modifier which goes with it. The verbal modifiers usually consist of (a) nonsentences (i.e. titles, labels, and legends) and/or (b) sentences (usually adjacent captions).[55] Thus :

A pictorial illustration ⟶ a picture + verbal modifiers.

5.3.2 As Hill pointed out in his article, "The typology of writing systems," pictures have played a great role in human communication and in the evolution of the symbolic representations of language.[56] In modern education, John Amos Comenius (1592-1670), was the first one who emphasized the use of pictorial illustrations in language learning. Many of his principles and techniques are still in use. His

---

[54] Malcolm Fleming, "Classification and analysis of instructional illustrations," *A V Communication Review*, 15 (1967), p. 247.

[55] *Ibid.*, p. 249.

[56] Archibald A. Hill, "The typology of writing systems," in *Papers in Linguistics in Honor of Leon Dostert*, ed. by William A. Austin (The Hague : Mouton, 1967). pp. 93-94.

bilingual book, *Orbis Pictus* (The World Illustrated), which appeared in 1657, contains pictures of things with brief sentences attached to each in an attempt to define all the words and phrases of Latin texts. There is, for instance, a picture of a ship with all its parts numbered. These numbers correspond to identically numbered sentences in the lesson. On the sails of the ship, there is a 2, and the lesson has the sentence, "The ship has (2) sails." The main purpose is to motivate children, who are usually delighted with pictures, to learn the target language.[57]

However, the use of pictorial illustrations has not found its way into European or American bilingual lexicographical tradition. In commercial monolingual dictionaries, the use of pictorial illustration is a recent addition. Older dictionaries used to depend solely on verbal definitions. Pictorial illustrations usually appear on separate plates, on foldout sheets, or alongside the printed texts. Their use is incidental and arbitrary. Pictorial illustrations certainly add to the size and cost of the dictionary, and it seems that no editor is certain whether they add proportionately to the user's benefit. When the editors of *Webster's Third New International* wanted to accommodate approximately 100,000 new words and word meanings, which had not been recorded in the second edition, they reduced the color plates and illustrations somewhere between one fourth and one third.[58] This shows that the importance of pictorial illustration is not taken seriously. The use of pictorial illustrations is rarely dealt with in the literature on lexicography, and the few references to it suffer from serious misconceptions. One of Malkiel's very few references to pictorial illustrations in his elaborate typology of dictionaries reads :

> ...historical slant and profusion of pictorial illustrations do not go together : maps, sketches, drawings, and photographs befit the synchronic dictionary, geographically oriented.[59]

The weakness of this statement is obvious since it is quite helpful to use drawings and photographs in the historical dictionary to illustrate the culture items which no longer exist and which the user cannot easily conceive without the aid of pictorial illustrations. By the same token, maps fit beautifully in a historical dictionary because they save

---

[57] S. S. Laurie, *John Amos Comenius : His Life and Educational Works* (Cambridge : The University Press, 1904), pp. 223-224.

[58] Albert H. Marckwardt, "Dictionaries and the English language," p. 340.

[59] Yakov Malkiel, "A typological classification of dictionaries on the basis of distinctive features," in Householder and Saporta, p. 23.

the many words that would be needed to describe old political and geographical borders. In a recent article, Malkiel expressed the view that a pictorial illustration "befits an encyclopedia rather than a dictionary."[60]

The present writer holds that pictorial illustrations should be systematically and consistently employed in bilingual dictionaries, not for the purpose of advertisement, but as an essential lexicographic device. This section is devoted to discussing the major aspects of this issue.

5.3.3 Pictorial illustrations can serve two functions in the bilingual dictionary :

(a) They cue and reinforce the verbal equivalents, especially when the dictionary user can identify, attend to, and respond differentially to the picture.

(b) They serve as generalizing examples when several different but relevant pictures are given in order to establish the concept they are intended to illustrate.[61]

According to Smith, pictorial illustrations help the dictionary user understand and remember the content of the accompanying verbal equivalent because they motivate him, reinforce what is read, and symbolically enhance and deepen the meaning of the verbal equivalent.[62, 63]

Two questions might be raised in this connection :

(a) Can pictorial illustrations be employed in the dictionary on a large scale?

(b) How useful are the pictorial illustrations if the dictionary user is not familiar with the object pictured?

The first question is raised because, although pictures can illustrate actions and objects, they are usually used in dictionaries with nouns, specifically concrete nouns, not the abstract ones. And so one may

---

[60] Yakov Malkiel, "Lexicography," in *The Learning of Language*, ed. by Carroll E. Reed (New York : Appleton-Century-Crofts, 1971), p. 377.

[61] G. L. Gropper, "Why is a picture worth a thousand words?" *A V Communication Review*, 11 (1963), pp. 76-77.

[62] Karl U. Smith, "The scientific principles of textbook design and illustration," *A V Communication Review*, 8 (1960), p. 29.

[63] For contrary point of view see M. D. Vernon, "The use of graphic material with a written text," abstracted in *A V Communication Review*, 4 (1957), 565. She challenged the usefulness of pictorial illustrations on the grounds that their interpretation requires special training, and the user often misinterprets the picture. Vernon's research suffered from several limitations and her objection can be met if the quality of the pictorial illustrations employed in the dictionary is improved.

think that pictorial illustrations can be used only on a very small scale. But this is not the case. Statistical studies show that nouns form a relatively high percentage of the language in comparison with the other parts of speech. Table 2 shows the relative size of the four major parts of speech in English and French at the thousand-word level :

Table 2[64]

Part of Speech	English	French
Nouns	41.9%	50.7%
Verbs	26.9%	30.5%
Adjectives	18.3%	15.2%
Adverbs	12.9%	3.6%
Total	100.0%	100.0%

Therefore, pictorial illustrations can be employed with more words than one might assume.

The second question raises the philosophical problem of "pictorial perception," i.e. how pictures are perceived. There are two theories about this. The stimulus theory states that perception is the product of the stimulus properties, whereas the introverted theory emphasizes the role of the perceiver, especially his past experiences, in the perception of pictures. Linker accepted a combination of both theories when he said :

> The perception of a picture is the product of both the stimulus properties of that picture and the past experiences of the perceiver.[65]

The two theories can be taken not as opposing each other but as complementary to each other. When the perceiver is familiar with the object pictured, his past experiences play an important role in the process of perception. But when the object pictured is new to the perceiver, then it is the stimulus properties of the picture which will be a determining factor in the formation of the concept. Accordingly, pictorial illustrations can be employed in the bilingual dictionary to illustrate objects familiar to the user as well as those culture items which are peculiar to the foreign language.

---

[64] Summarized from William Francis MacKey, *Language Teaching Analysis* (Bloomington : Indiana Univ. Press, 1967), p. 168.

[65] Jerry Mac Linker, *The Interaction of Cognitive Factors, Visual Fidelity, and Learning Tasks in Learning from Pictures* (Unpublished Ph. D. Thesis, University of Texas, 1971), p. 12.

5.3.4 The use of pictorial illustrations should not be arbitrary or incidental; but rather subjected to certain objective considerations. The most important considerations in this connection are :

(1) Pictorial illustrations should be used whenever they possess more discriminable properties, as well as when they have more control over the desired concept or over potentially competing concepts than do their verbal equivalents.[66] In other words, the lexicographer should employ a pictorial illustration when it can univocally cue and reinforce a particular response or establish a particular concept more efficiently than could a verbal equivalent alone.

(2) Pictorial illustrations should be used when the verbal equivalent requires an uneconomical number of words. In such cases a brief definition or a short explanatory equivalent may be supplemented by a pictorial illustration which gives the dictionary user a fuller understanding of the concept defined.

(3) Pictorial illustrations should be used when verbal equivalents cannot show spatial or sequential relationships effectively. Such graphic aids as charts, maps, and diagrams may prove more efficient than words in facilitating the acquisition of relational concepts. In the words of Gropper :

> Visual portrayal of some kinds of relationships may be more effective in this regard than words because of the visual's spatial or sequential properties. Many relevant cues about complex relationships can be more briefly presented both typographically and temporally.[67]

5.3.5 The lexicographer should have substantial knowledge about pictorial illustrations as necessary components of his dictionary. He should know their physical and behavioral attributes and the essential principles of designing pictures for lexicographical undertakings. The following are criteria for ideal pictorial illustrations :

(1) Compactness :

The human eye is capable of transmitting a very large amount of information, sometimes more than the brain can process. Therefore, it is necessary to reduce the pictorial illustration to its essentials. Since not all bits of information are of equal importance, irrelevant information (i.e. information which is not specifically relevant to the concept illustrated) should be kept to the minimum, and visual noise (i.e. information which distracts the dictionary user from correct

---

[66] Gropper, "Why is a picture worth a thousand words?" p. 80.
[67] *Ibid.*, p. 81.

interpretation or recognition of the pictorial illustration) must be strictly eliminated.[68]

(2) Fidelity :

Fidelity of pictorial illustrations is closely related to how realistic they are. It is generally assumed that photographic detail and realistic color increase the fidelity of pictorial illustration. However, experimental studies on the value of photographic detail as compared to drawings, and of realistic color as compared to black and white have produced inconsistent results.[69, 70] However, the type of pictorial illustration (i.e. realistic or abstract) is usually determined by the nature of the subject matter and the level of the behavioral objective. The higher the behavioral objective is, the more abstract the pictorial illustration should be.[71]

(3) Interpretability :

By interpretability is meant here that the pictorial illustration can be interpreted by the dictionary user, i.e. he can understand the message conveyed by the picture. Interpretability has the following components:

(i) Relevance : Since all illustrations involve some kind of abstraction, pictures should be related to the user's past environmental and realistic experiences which are determining factors in his success in the interpretation of the picture. Spaulding made the following recommendations :

> ...when preparing material for children or for foreign audiences, the artist must attempt to construct the pictorial image in terms of an audience whose background is much more limited and/or couched in a different cultural setting than his own.[72]

This does not imply that illustrations of objects unfamiliar to the user cannot be employed in the bilingual dictionary. "In such cases," Spaulding recommended, "care must be taken to use the visual construction in careful context with other illustrative and textual material..."[73]

---

[68] Linker, *op. cit.*, p. 27.

[69] L. C. Twyford, "Educational communications media," in *The Encyclopedia of Educational Research*, 4th ed., ed. by R. L. Ebel (Boston : The Macmillan Co., 1969), pp. 367-369.

[70] Linker, *op. cit.*, pp. 30-32.

[71] Malcolm Fleming, "Classification and analysis of instructional illustrations," pp. 257-258.

[72] Seth Spaulding, "Communication potential of pictorial illustration," *A V Communication Review*, 4 (1956), p. 45.

[73] *Ibid.*

(ii) Simplicity : The pictorial illustration should require a minimum of separate actions on the part of the dictionary user to interpret its basic message.[74] Simplicity also implies that the pictorial illustration should not be open to dual interpretation resulting from a complex pictorial illustration (i.e. one which involves many discriminations).[75]

(iii) Preciseness : The dictionary user's attention should be directed only to the feature of the pictorial illustration relevant to the desired concept. The most effective attention directing and modifying devices are :

(a) arrows indicating the points of interest in the picture.
(b) reduction of irrelevant information in the pictorial illustration.
(c) color cues to indicate the most important feature of the picture.
(d) position cues which imply that the most important portion of the picture should be placed in the center or upper left of the illustration.
(e) identifying numbers which correspond to verbal modifiers such as titles and captions.

(iv) Completeness : The title and caption should be complete and add something descriptive to the picture in order to facilitate its interpretation. The title should identify the picture, otherwise it might be taken as an illustration of an adjacent entry or a neighboring sense. The caption should add information which is difficult to depict.[76] Usually, pictorial illustrations prepared to serve high level objectives require more verbal modifiers. In the words of Fleming :

> The level of difficulty of the objective assigned to each illustration was positively related to the number of types of verbal modifiers and to the overall number of verbal modifiers associated with the illustration.[77]

(v) Clarity : The features of the pictorial illustrations should be easily distinguished by the dictionary user. This requires an adequate artistic and typographical performance and an appropriate size (the minimum is $2'' \times 3''$).

The points raised in this section are intended as points of departure for the use of pictorial illustrations in bilingual lexicography. Further research is recommended.

---

[74] *Ibid.*

[75] Gropper, "Why is a picture worth a thousand words?" p. 80.

[76] Seth Spaulding, "Research on pictorial illustration," *A V Communication Review*, 3 (1955), p. 44.

[77] Malcolm Fleming, "Classification and analysis of instructional illustrations," p. 257.

5.4   Bilingual Lexicography and Foreign Language Teaching

5.4.1   Although the earliest English bilingual dictionaries were prepared as an aid to the learners of foreign languages especially Latin, French, and Spanish, nowadays many teachers are reluctant to use bilingual dictionaries. Their attitude is a product of the philosophy underlying the Direct Method which was a strong reaction to the Grammar-translation approach. As Catford pointed out, "there are still devoted followers of the 'Direct Method' who regard any use of translation in language-teaching as, almost, immoral."[78] Consequently, they tell students not to use bilingual dictionaries because they are of minimal value and they give the wrong impression that there is a one-to-one correspondence between the student's native language and the target language. However, recent psycholinguistic research has proven that the adequate use of translation is sometimes necessary in sound foreign-language teaching. Rivers, who reviewed the psychological literature on this issue, concluded :

> Much as we might like to exclude from the learning of the foreign language all influence of native language, this is impossible. By accepting the inevitable, we can use the elements of native-language learning which will help foreign-language learning, such as learned ability to imitate sounds, understanding of functions of words, elements of patterning which are for practical purposes identical in the two languages, existing concepts which are similar to the new concepts, and reading skill, thus reducing to some degree the time necessary for learning the new language.[79]

What is dangerous in foreign-language teaching is not the use of the native language, but the misuse of it. Translation may be used in the foreign-language classroom for the initial presentation of meaning and the consolidation of learning by checking on the student's comprehension.[80]

Dividing foreign-language learning into three stages, elementary, intermediate, and advanced, the present writer can justify the use of bilingual dictionaries in all of these stages :

(a) The elementary stage : Although meanings are presented by many teachers in situational context, a glossary or footnotes are useful in the textbook for they serve as a kind of reference to the student.

---

[78] J.C. Catford, "Translation and language teaching," in *Linguistic Theories and their Applications* (London : AIDELA, 1967), p. 125.

[79] Wilga M. Rivers, *The Psychologist and the Foreign Language Teacher* (Chicago : The University of Chicago Press, 1964), p. 126.

[80] Catford, *op. cit.*, p. 142.

In language textbooks, glossaries and footnotes can be considered as lexicographical work.

(b) The intermediate stage: In addition to the use of glossaries in the foreign-language textbooks, the student needs a good bilingual dictionary to help him in his reading of simplified materials in the foreign language. Monolingual dictionaries in the target language cannot be fruitfully employed in this stage because the student does not always understand definitions which use special lexicographical language and conventions, or which include words he does not know. Sometimes the student cannot form the proper concept even if he understands the meanings of the individual words of a definition; in other words he cannot understand the "structural meaning" of the definition. A good bilingual dictionary is an indispensable tool for the student in the intermediate stage of foreign-language learning.

(c) The advanced stage: First of all, the student should use monolingual dictionaries prepared especially for foreign students. Later on he can use some good monolingual dictionary. But monolingual dictionaries can help the learner in comprehension only. For production, whether speaking or writing, the student has to use a bilingual dictionary.

5.4.2 Very few linguists have concerned themselves with the criteria for a good dictionary to use in learning languages. In a pioneer effort in this field 29 years ago, Hill published an article, "The use of dictionaries in language teaching,"[81] in which he laid the basis for the sound use of dictionaries in the teaching of English, both as a native language and as a second language. The five kinds of information Hill assigned to the ideal dictionary are still, and will always be, essential, not only in a dictionary prepared for pedagogical purposes, but in any other dictionary as well. These five types of information are: "the phonemic structure of the word, its morphemic structure, the grammatical modifications it undergoes, its syntactic habits, and its meanings."[82] Having done extensive research on the use of dictionaries in language teaching, Yorkey concluded, in an article published recently, that the criteria for choosing a good dictionary should be different for foreign students of the language and for native speakers.[83]

---

[81] Archibald A. Hill, "The use of dictionaries in language teaching," *Language Learning*, 1 (1948), pp. 9-13.

[82] *Ibid.*, p. 10.

[83] Richard Yorkey, "Which desk dictionary is best for foreign students of English?" *TESOL Quarterly*, 3 (1969), p. 257.

Yorkey's criteria for choosing a good dictionary for foreign students of English are: 1. simple pronunciation symbols, 2. the indication of hyphenation, 3. easy definitions, 4. the inclusion of current campus usage, 5. the inclusion of idioms, phrases, and two-word verbs, 6. labeling of language levels, 7. the inclusion of cultural references, and 8. good editorial matter including a grammar of the language, tables of weights and measures, and the like.[84]

One of the major problems in the making of dictionaries for language teaching is the selection of words and meanings. Selection should depend on adequate sampling of the target language. If the sample is too large, it will duplicate the materials available in the unabridged dictionaries, and if it is too small, it will not be accurate.[85] The sample should always aim at bringing the record of the language up-to-date. The principal criteria for the selection of entries and meanings are: (a) frequency, based on both frequency count and semantic count, (b) usefulness, and (c) restriction to the regional and social dialects which the dictionary purports to record.[86] Although "it does not seem that it is the duty of the lexicographer to collect all instances of genuine figures of speech," as Hill pointed out,[87] the glossary of a language textbook should include all the figures of speech occurring in that textbook.

Another problem pertaining to the use of bilingual dictionaries in language teaching is the inclusion of etymology. Some feel that the etymologies of the foreign words should be included;[88] others believe that etymologies are "of little or no concern to the language learners," who are untrained in the intricacies of historical grammar.[89] The present writer here proposes a new type of etymology for bilingual dictionaries in general and for those used in language teaching in particular. The bilingual dictionary should provide etymological information only about those foreign words which are borrowed from or by the user's native language. This will certainly facilitate learning and increase the learner's interest.

---

[84] *Ibid.*, pp. 257-270.

[85] C. L. Barnhart, "Problems in editing commercial monolingual dictionaries," in Householder and Saporta, p. 167.

[86] Yakov Malkiel, "Lexicography," in *The Learning of Language*, ed. by Carroll E. Reed (New York: Appleton-Century-Crofts, 1970), p. 366.

[87] Archibald A. Hill, "Principles governing semantic parallels," *Studies in Literature and Language*, 1 (1959), p. 359.

[88] Al-Ba'labakki, *Al-Mawrid: A Modern English-Arabic Dictionary*, p. iii.

[89] Malkiel, "Lexicography," p. 379.

Another problem is how to provide phonological information in the bilingual dictionary employed in language teaching. Recognizing that any transcription system would add new difficulties for the language learner, in addition to its inaccurate representation of all the features of the target language, Michel of the University of Texas proposes a new method to solve the problem. It should be pointed out that Michel's proposal would require a substantial change in the format of the dictionary and it is meant primarily for reference dictionaries to be available in schools and libraries. The new method requires that each entry of a dictionary be recorded on a card which contains all the necessary information such as meaning, grammar, pictorial illustrations, and illustrative examples. The card also has a sound track on which the word and its illustrative examples are recorded. The cards are alphabetically arranged in a catalogue. The language learner looks the word up in the catalogue, takes the card out, studies the information, and inserts the card in a language master (which is really a recording machine) placed next to the catalogue. When the card moves through the card slot, the student hears the word pronounced in isolation then in one or more illustrative examples. The student can listen to the card as many times as he wishes, and he can even practice the pronunciation of the recorded material by holding the listen/record lever of the machine in the "record" position for the duration of his recording sequence. In this way, he can compare his pronunciation with that of the master tape.[90]

One of the problems pertaining to monolingual dictionaries intended for the foreign learners is the language of their definitions. Definitions should use easy words and constructions so that the reader will understand them without much difficulty. Dr. Johnson was well aware of the problem when he said :

> To explain requires the use of terms less abstruse than that which is to be explained, and such terms cannot always be found;...[91]

One way to handle this problem is to reduce the defining vocabulary to the minimum. West and Endicott, for example, used a vocabulary of only 1490 words in the definitions of the 24,000 words and idioms listed in *The New Method English Dictionary*, which was written

---

[90] Joseph Michel, Lectures on Foreign Language Teaching at the University of Texas at Austin, Spring 1972. A similar idea has been recently put into practice by Bell & Howell Company which produced a "talking dictionary" series.

[91] Samuel Johnson, *A Dictionary of the English Language*, p. 6.

specially for the foreigner.[92] A similar technique seems to have been
adopted in the preparation of *The Advanced Learner's Dictionary*.[93]

5.4.3 Language teachers should provide their students with lexicographical education. The neglect of this important aspect of linguistic
education results not only in the student's inefficient use of dictionaries
but in many misconceptions about their nature and function. Commenting on the controversy about *Webster's Third New International*,
Marckwardt said :

> It is the English-teaching profession which should be seriously disturbed
> by the dictionary controversy. If the Webster war has proved little or
> nothing about dictionaries, it has demonstrated our ineptitude, if not
> absolute failure, in teaching our students what a dictionary is for, how
> it is made, and the proper way to use it. Much of the misunderstanding of
> principle, of the confusion of principle and practice, of the failure to read
> and interpret accurately can, with considerable justice, be laid at our
> door....[94]

A sound lexicographical education should include the following
features :

(a) The students should be lectured briefly on the history of the
foreign language they are learning and its relation to other languages,
its progenitors as well as its descendants.

(b) The teacher should explain to his students the prescriptive and
descriptive trends in dictionary making. He should point out that
modern linguistics indicates that a lexicographer is a historian not
a linguistic legislator; his duty is to record usage, not to invent it.

(c) The students should be given brief sketches of the major dictionaries available in the library, of the circumstances under which each
dictionary was made, and of the characteristics and excellencies of
each.

(d) Since dictionaries are tools of instruction as well as information,
and "they are much more complicated, and capable of more uses than
students suspect,"[95] the students should learn how to use them
efficiently and effectively. He should learn to study the front matter
to acquaint himself with the compiler's design, abbreviations, symbols,

---

[92] Michel Philip West and James Gareth Endicott, *The New English Dictionary*
(London : Longmans, 1935), p. iii.

[93] A. S. Hornby, E. V. Gatenby and H. Wakefield, *The Advanced Learner's Dictionary*
(London : Oxford University Press, 1948).

[94] Marckwardt, "Dictionaries and the English language," pp. 344-345.

[95] Mitford M. Mathews, "The freshman and his dictionary," in *Readings in Applied
Linguistics*, ed. by Harold B. Allen (New York : Appleton-Century-Crofts, 1964), p. 435.

and other lexicographical conventions. Just finding a word in a dictionary does not mean that the student can understand the information provided about it.

In short, the selection of a good dictionary is not sufficient in itself; the user should have the necessary lexicographical education which enables him to get the most out of that dictionary. And it is the duty of the language teacher to provide his students with that education.

CONCLUSIONS AND CRITERIA

The conclusions of this study are put in the form of a set of criteria for preparing, selecting, or evaluating bilingual dictionaries. The criteria cover three major aspects : purpose, content, and format.

I   *Purpose*

1.1   Oneness of purpose :
1.11   Is the dictionary intended to serve the speakers of the source language, or the speakers of the target language?
1.12   Is the dictionary dealing primarily with the written language or the spoken language?
1.13   Is the dictionary prepared as an aid in comprehension or production?

1.2   Modernity :
1.21   Does the dictionary register the vocabulary of recent cultural developments such as "telstar," "busing," and "videotape recorder?"
1.22   Are the recent findings of modern linguistics in phonology, grammar, and semantics applied in the dictionary?

II   *Content*

2.1   The front matter :
2.11   Introduction : Does the introduction indicate the following?
       (a)   the purpose of the dictionary,
       (b)   the sources of the dictionary,
       (c)   the method of compilation,
       (d)   the grammatical philosophy which underlies the dictionary,
       (e)   coverage : lexical items and word senses,
       (f)   the types of information provided.
2.12   History of the language : Is there a history of the target language showing its development and its relations to other languages?
2.13   The sound system of the target language :
       (a)   Is there a systematic presentation of the phonemes of the language and the distribution of their allophones?

(b)   Is there a pronunciation guide illustrating the transcription system adopted in the dictionary?

(c)   Is there a key to the pronunciation citing two or three familiar words as examples to each symbol?

2.14 The grammar of the target language :

(a)   Does the grammar include an outline of the morphological and syntactical systems of the target language setting up distinct categories (and subcategories) and the relationships between them?

(b)   Is there a systematic exemplified presentation of the devices of derivation such as compounding, suffixation, zero change, and reduplication?

2.15 Writing : Does the front matter include an outline of the writing system of the target language, the spelling rules and their exceptions?

2.16 A guide to the dictionary : Is there a guide to the proper use of the dictionary indicating abbreviations, lexicographical conventions, and special techniques employed in it?

2.2   The body of the dictionary :

2.21 Form :

(a)   Spelling : Are various spellings of each word entered alphabetically in their proper place with cross-reference to the main entry?

(b)   Hyphenation : Does the dictionary employ any adequate device (hyphens or periods) within the entry words to indicate points at which a word can be cut at the end of a written or typed line?

2.22 Entries :

(a)   Do the dictionary entries include morphemes as well as morphemic sequences?

(b)   Do they cover the subject-matter adequately?

(c)   Do they include idioms, and two-word verbs?

(d)   Do they include culture items such as proper names of persons, places, and literary works?

2.23 Phonological information :

(a)   Are the entry word and its illustrative examples transcribed?

(b)   Is the transcription system employed in the dictionary simple, complete, and accurate?

(c)   Does the transcription system employed in the dictionary indicate the suprasegmental phonemes as well as the segmental ones?

2.24   Grammatical information : Does the dictionary indicate
   (a)   The morphological structure of the entry?
   (b)   All the changes the entry word undergoes such as tenses, cases, and gender?
   (c)   The syntactic behavior of the entry word?

2.25   Semantic information :
   (a)   Are all the major senses of the word listed?
   (b)   Does the dictionary aim at citing one adequate translational equivalent to each sense?
   (c)   Are there linguistic and cultural notes attached to the equivalents wherever necessary?
   (d)   Are meaning discriminations provided in the user's language where needed?
   (e)   Is the relationship between derivatives of the same word family indicated?

2.26   Usage :
   (a)   Are linguistic usage labels such as "formal," "informal" and "poetic" used accurately?
   (b)   Does the dictionary employ social labels such as "derogatory," "offensive," and "not among women?"

2.27   Illustrative examples :
   (a)   Is each sense illustrated with a quotation?
   (b)   Do quotations represent the culture of the speakers of the target language?
   (c)   Are all quotations translated into the user's native language?
   (d)   Are quotations brief and informative, i.e. illustrating the usage of the word?

2.28   Pictorial illustrations :
   (a)   Are pictorial illustrations employed systematically, i.e. whenever they add information to or express the meaning more explicitly than the verbal equivalent?
   (b)   Are pictorial illustrations realistic and interpretable?

2.29   Etymology : Are borrowings from or by the user's native language pointed out in the dictionary?

2.3   Appendices : Are there any appendices providing commonly sought information about the target language culture such as

    (a)   currency,
    (b)   weights and measures,
    (c)   thermometer system,
    (d)   lists of major educational and political institutions,
    (e)   maps.

III   *Format :* *

    (a)   Does the dictionary have an eye-pleasing and attractive format?
    (b)   Are the pages well-printed and the entries in bold face?
    (c)   Are typographical errors kept to the minimum?

---

* Format has not been discussed in this book.

BIBLIOGRAPHY

Abboud, Peter F. "Spoken Arabic," in *Current Trends in Linguistics Vol. 6 : Linguistics in South West Asia and North Africa*, ed. by Thomas A. Sebeok. (The Hague : Mouton, 1971,) 439-466.

Aḥmad, 'Abdul-Samī' M. *Al-Ma'ājim Al-'arabiyah* (Cairo : Dāru'l-Fikr al-'arabi, 1969).

Al-Kasimi, Ali M. *Mukhtabaru 'l-Lughah* (Kuwait : Daru'l-Qalam, 1970).

——, "Review of Al-Mawrid : A Modern English-Arabic Dictionary," in *Papers Presented to Archibald A. Hill by His Students*, ed. by Ali M. Al-Kasimi et al. (Austin, 1971) mimeographed.

Al-Khaṭīb, 'Adnān. *Al-Mu'jam Al-'Arabī bayna Al-Madhī Walḥādhir.* (Cairo : Ma'hadu 'l-Buḥuθ Wa-l-dirāsāt Al-'Arabiyah, 1967).

Allen, Harold B., et al. "Webster's Third New International Dictionary : a symposium," *The Quarterly Journal of Speech*, 48 (1962), 431-440. [Including also Margaret M. Bryant, Robert A. Hall, Jr., Raven I. McDavid, Jr., John B. Newman, Allen Walker Read, and Robert Sonkin.]

Allen, Robert L. "The structure of meaning," in *Proceedings of the Ninth International Congress of Linguists*, ed. by H. Lunt (The Hague : Mouton & Co., 1964), 421-426.

Antal, L. "A new type of dictionary," *Linguistics*, 1 (1963), 75-84.

Bailey, Richard W. "Review of the American Heritage Dictionary," *Language Sciences*, 10 (1970), 23-29.

——, and Jay L. Robinson. "The computer in lexicography." Paper presented to the Midwest Modern Language Association, October 24, 1969, mimeographed.

Bar-Hillel, Yehoshua. "Idioms," in *Machine Translation of Languages* ed. by William N. Locke and A. Donald Booth, 183-193. (Cambridge : Technology Press, 1955).

Barnhart, Clarence L. "Contributions of Dr. Thorndike to lexicography," *Teachers College Record*, 51, (1949), 35-42.

——, "Problems in editing commercial monolingual dictionaries," in Householder and Saporta, 161-181.

Barzun, Jacques. "What is a dictionary?" *American Scholar*, 32 (1963), 176-181.

Bendix, Edward H. "Componential analysis of general vocabulary : the semantic structure of a set of verbs in English, Hindi, and Japanese," *International Journal of American Linguistics*, 32/2 (1966).

Besterman, T. "On a bibliography of dictionaries," in *The Proceedings of the British Society for International Bibliography*, IV (London, 1943), 63-73.

Bishop, Morris "Good usage, bad usage, and usage," in *The American Heritage Dictionary* ed. by William Morris (Boston : American Heritage Publishing Co., 1969), xxi-xxiv.

Blachère, Régis; Chouémi, Moustafa; and Denizeau, Claude. *Dictionnaire Arabe-Français-Anglais* (Paris : G.-P. Maisonneuve et Larose, 1967).

Black, Max, "Linguistic relativity : the views of Benjamin Lee Whorf," *Model and Metaphors*. (Ithaca, N.Y. : Cornell University Press, 1962), 244-257.

Bloomfield, Leonard. "Linguistics as a science," *Studies in Philology*, 27 (1930), 553-557.

——, *Language* (New York : Holt, Rinehart & Winston, 1933).

——, "Language or ideas?" *Language*, 12 (1936), 89-95.

——, "Meaning," *Monatshefte*, 35 (1943), 101-106.

Bolinger, Dwight. *Aspects of Language* (New York : Harcourt, Brace & World, 1968). [On "The Dictionary," 286-292.]

——, "The atomization of meaning," *Language*, 41 (1965), 555-573.

Brake, Stillman. "Back from limbo: the rediscovery of Alexander Bryan Johnson," in *Language and Value*, ed. by Charles L. Todd and Russell T. Blackwood, (New York: Greenwood Publ. Corp., 1969), 3-15.

Bréal, Michel. *Semantics: Studies in the Science of Meaning.* trans. by Mrs. Henry Cust (London: Heinemann, 1900).

Bright, William. "Language and culture," *International Encyclopedia of the Social Sciences*, ed. by David L. Sills, 9, 18-22. (New York: Crowell Collier, 1968).

Bronstein, Arthur. "The pronunciation of English," in *The Random House Dictionary of the English Language*, ed. by Jess Stein (New York: Random House, 1966), xxiii-xxiv.

Bruke, W. J., The Literature of Slang (1939) (New York: New York Public Library, 1939) Reprinted 1965, Detroit: Gale.

Brumbaugh, James E. "Review of A Classified Dictionary of Spoken Manchu by Kengo Yamamoto," *Language*, 47 (1971), 910-975.

Bull, William E. "The use of vernacular languages in education," [Review of *The Use of Vernacular Languages in Education* (Monograph on Fundamental Education, No. 8) Paris: UNESCO, 1953.], in *Language in Culture and Society*, ed. by Dell Hymes (New York: Harper & Row, Publishers, 1964), 527-533.

Burling, R. "Cognition and componential analysis," *American Anthropologist*, 1 (1964), 20-28.

Burrill, Meredith F., and Bonsack, Edwin, Jr. "Use and preparation of specialized glossaries," in Householder and Saporta, 183-199.

Cameron, Angus, John Leyerle, and Roberta Frank, (eds.) *Computers and Old English Concordances* (Toronto: University of Toronto Press, 1970).

Carnap, R. "Meaning and synonymy in natural languages," *Philosophical Studies*, 7 (1955), 33-47.

Cary, E. and R. W. Jumpelt (eds.) *Quality in Translation*: Proceedings of the IIIrd Congress of the International Federation of Translators (FIT) (New York: The Macmillan Co., 1963).

Casagrande, Joseph, and Kenneth Hale. "Semantic relationship in Papago folk definitions," in *Studies in Southwestern Ethnolinguistics*, ed. by Dell Hymes. (The Hague: Mouton, 1967), 165-196.

Cassidy, Frederic G. "On collecting American dialect." *American Speech*, 23 (1948), 185-93.

——, "On the scope of the American Dialect Society's dictionary." Report of the second conference on planning for the dictionary of the American Dialect Society, 5-11. (Tulsa: University of Tulsa, 1950).

——, "A method for collecting dialect." *Publications of the American Dialect Society*, 20 (1953), 1-96.

——, "The ADS dictionary—how soon?" *Publications of the American Dialect Society*, 39 (1963), 1-7.

——, "A descriptive approach to lexicon," in *Approaches in Linguistic Methodology*, ed. by Irmengard Rauch and Charles T. Scott (Madison: University of Wisconsin Press, 1967), 9-15.

——, and R. B. Le Page. "Lexicographical problems of the dictionary of Jamaican English," *Proceedings of the Conference on Creole Language Studies* (1961), 17-36 = *Creole Language Studies*, 2, ed. by R. B. Le Page (London: Macmillan, 1961).

Catford, J. C. *A Linguistic Theory of Translation* (London: Oxford University Press, 1965).

——, "Translation and language teaching," in *Linguistic Theories and their Application* (London: International Association of Publishers of Applied Linguistics, 1967), 125-146.

Chafe, Wallace L. *Meaning and the Structure of Language.* (Chicago: University of Chicago Press, 1970).

Chapin, Paul G. "Linguistic semantics today," *English Record*, 20 (1970), 49-66.
Chapman, Robert William. *Johnsonian and Other Essays and Reviews*. (Oxford : Clarendon Press, 1953).
——, *Lexicography* (London : New York : Oxford University Press, 1948).
——, *Two Centuries of Johnsonian Scholarship* (Glasgow : Jackson, Son & Co., 1945).
Chatman, Seymour, "Review of Speculative Instruments by I. A. Richards," *Language*, 33 (1957), 505-518.
Chavarria-Aguilar, O. L., and Penzl, Herbert. "Lexicographical problems in Pashto," in Householder and Saporta, 237-247.
Chomsky, Noam, *Aspects of the Theory of Syntax* (Cambridge : M.I.T. Press, 1965).
——, Deep structure, surface structure, and semantic interpretation," in *Semantics*, ed by Danny D. Steinberg and Leon A. Jakobovits (Cambridge : Cambridge University Press, 1971), 183-216.
——, "Remarks on nominalization," in *Readings in English Transformational Grammar*, ed. by Roderick A. Jacobs and Peter S. Rosenbaum (Waltham, Massachusetts : Gin and Company, 1970), 184-221.
——, "Semantic considerations in grammar," *Monograph Series on Languages and Linguistics*, 8 (1955), 141-153.
——, *Syntactic Structures* (The Hague : Mouton, 1957).
Citroen, I. J. (ed.) *Ten Years of Translation : Proceedings of the Fourth Congress of the International Federation of Translators (FIT)* (Oxford : Pergamon Press, 1967).
Clardi, John. "What is a dictionary?" *Saturday Review* (7 June 1969), 12-13.
Coates, William Ames. "Meaning in morphemes and compound lexical units," *Proceedings of the International Congress of Linguists*, IX (1964), 1046-51.
Cohen, Gerald. "How did the English word 'just' acquire its different meanings?" *Papers from the Fifth Regional Meeting of the Chicago Linguistic Society*. (Chicago : Dept. of Linguistics, University of Chicago, 1969), 25-29.
Cohen, M. "Compléments de verbes et dictionnaires," in *Mélanges Jordan* (Bucarest, 1960), 173-181.
——, "Le fait dictionnaire," in *Proceedings of the Ninth International Congress of Linguists* (The Hague : Mouton, 1964), 497-503.
——, "Parlons un peu dictionnaires," in *L'Humanité*, 27 March, 1967.
Conklin, H. C. "Lexicographical treatment of folk taxonomies," in Householder and Saporta, 119-141.
Cook, Daniel. "A point of lexicographical method," *American Speech*, 34 (1959), 20-25.
Coseriu, E. "Les structures lexématiques," in *Probleme der Semantik*, ed. by T. Elwert, Zeitschrift für Französische Sprache und Literatur, Franz Steiner Verlag GMBH, (Wiesbaden, 1968), 3-16.
Coteanu, I. "Le dictionnaire de la langue roumaine (D.L.R.)," *Revue Roumaine de Linguistique*, X (1965), 31-43.
Council for Cultural Co-operation of the Council of Europe. *Linguistic Theories and their Application*. (London : AIDELA, 1967).
Darbelnet, J. "Dictionnaires bilingues et lexicologie différentielle," *Langages*, No. 19 (Sept., 1970), 92-102.
Darwīsh, 'Abdullāh. *Al-Ma'ājim Al-'Arabiyah* (Cairo : Maktabatu'l-Anglo Al-Miṣrīyah, 1956).
Diebold, A. Richard. "Review of Psycholinguistics, ed. by Sol Saporta," *Language*, 40 (1964), 197-260.
Dinneen, F. *An Introduction to General Linguistics* (New York : Holt, Rinehart & Winston, Inc., 1967).
Dixon, R. M. "A trend in semantics," *Linguistics*, 1 (1963), 30-57.
Drysdale, Patrick. "Lexicography : statics and dynamics," *Canadian Journal of Linguistics*, 14 (1969), 108-122.

Dubois, J. "Dictionnaire et discours didactique," *Langages*, No. 19 (Sept. 1970), 35-47.

——, "Esquisse d'un dictionnaire structural," *Études de Linguistique Appliquée*, 1 (1962), 43-48.

——, "Le mot : règles lexicographiques d'usage courant," *A.T.A.L.A. Collogue du 8 décembre 1962 (dactylographié)*.

——, "Pourquoi des dictionnaires?" *Information sur les Sciences Sociales*, VI (1967), 101-112.

——, "Les problèmes du vocabulaire technique," *Cahiers de Lexicologie*, II (1966), 104-112.

——, "Recherches lexicographiques : esquisse d'un dictionnaire structural," *Études de Linguistique Appliquée*, 1 (1962), 43-48.

——, "Représentation de systèmes paradigmatiques formalisés dans un dictionnaire structural," *Cahiers de Lexicologie*, II (1964), 3-15.

Dykema, Karl W. "Cultural lag and reviewers of Webster III," *AAUP Bulletin*, 49 (1963), 364-369.

Eaton, Helen S. *Semantic Frequency List for English, French, German and Spanish* (Chicago : Chicago University Press, 1940). [Reviewed by G. K. Lipfin in *American Speech*, 16 (1941), 43-45.]

Ebeling, C. L. *Linguistic Units* (The Hague : Mouton & Co., 1960).

Emery, Donald W. *Variant Spellings in Modern American Dictionaries*. (Champaign, Ill. : National Council of Teachers, 1958.)

Ervin, Susan, and Bower, R. T. "Translation Problems in International Surveys," *Public Opinion Quarterly*, 16, 4 : (1952) 595-604.

Esper, Erwin A. *Mentalism and Objectivism in Linguistics : The Sources of Leonard Bloomfield's Psychology of Language*. (Foundations of Linguistics, 1.) (New York : American Elsevier, 1968).

Ferguson, Charles A. "Diglossia," *Word*, 15 (1959), 325-340.

Fillmore, Charles J. "The grammar of hitting and breaking," in *Readings in English Transformational Grammar*, ed. by Roderick A. Jacobs and Peter S. Rosenbaum (Waltham, Mass.: Ginn and Company, 1970), 120-133.

——, "Types of lexical information," in *Working Papers in Linguistics No. 2* by C.J. Fillmore and Ilse Lehiste (Columbus, Ohio: Ohio State University, 1968), 65-103.

——, "Verbs of judging : an exercise in semantic description," in *Studies in Linguistic Semantics*, ed. by Charles J. Fillmore and D. Terence Langendoen (New York : Holt, Rinehart and Winston, Inc., 1971), 273-289.

Firth, J. R. "Linguistic analysis and translation," in *For Roman Jacobson*, ed. by Morris Halle (The Hague : Mouton, 1956), 133-139.

——, *Papers in Linguistics, 1934-1951*, (London : Oxford University Press, 1957).

Fishman, Joshua. "A systematization of the Whorfian hypothesis." *Behavioral Sciences*, 5 (1960), 323-339.

Fleming, Malcolm. "Classification and analysis of instructional illustrations," *A V Communication Review*, 15 (1967), 246-258.

Fodor, J. A., and Katz, J. J. (eds.) *The Structure of Language* (Englewoods Cliffs, N. J. : Prentice-Hall, 1964).

Fowler, R. "'Meaning' and the theory of the morpheme," *Lingua*, 12 (1963), 165-176.

(France). *Lexicologie et Lexicographie Françaises et Romanes*. (Strasbourg : Centre National de la Recherche Scientifique, 1961).

Francis, W. Nelson. *Manual of Information to Accompany a Standard Sample of Present-day Edited American English, for Use with Digital Computers*. (Providence, R. I. : Dept. of Linguistics, Brown University, 1964).

Fries, Charles C. "The Bloomfield 'School'," in *Trends in European and American Linguistics 1930-1960*, ed. by Christine Mohrmann, Alf Sommerfelt, and Joshua Whatmough (Utrecht, Netherlands : Spectrum Publishers, 1961), 196-224.

——, (with cooperation of A. Aileen Traver). *English Word Lists: A Study of Their Adaptability for Instruction* (Washington D. C. : American Council on Education, 1940).

——, "Meaning and linguistic analysis," *Language*, 30 (1954), 57-68.

——, "Preparation of teaching materials, practical grammars, and dictionaries, especially for foreign languages," in *Proceedings of the Eighth International Congress of Linguists* (Oslo, 1958), 738-745.

——, "Usage levels and dialect distribution," in *The American College Dictionary* ed. by C. L. Barnhart (New York : Random House, 1947), xxiv-xxvi.

Gak, V. G. "La langue et le discours dans un dictionnaire bilingue," *Langages*, No. 19 (Sept. 1970), 103-115.

Garvin, Paul L. "Problems in American Indian lexicography and text edition," *Anais do XXXI Congresso Internacional de Americanists*, São Paulo, 1955, 1013-1038.

——, Jocelyn Brewer, and Madeleine Mathiot. *Predication typing, a pilot study in semantic analysis*. [Language Monograph 27]. (Baltimore : LSA, 1967).

Gates, Edward. "Review of Glossary of Linguistic Terminology by Mario Pei," *Language*, 44 (1968), 317-326.

Gelb, I. J. "Lexicography, lexicology, and the Accadian dictionary," in *Á André Martinet Estructuralismo e Historia*, Vol. II, ed. by Diego Catalán (Canarias : Universidad de la Laguna, 1958) pp. 63-75.

Germanus, Abdul Karim. "Studies in Arabic lexicography," *The Islamic Quarterly*, 1 (1954), 12-28.

Gleason, H. A., Jr. "A file for a technical dictionary," *Monograph Series on Languages and Linguistics*, 14 (1961), 115-122.

——, "The relation of lexicon and grammar," in Householder and Saporta, 85-102.

——, *Linguistics and English Grammar* (New York : Holt, Rinehart and Winston, Inc., 1965.)

——, "Review of Gedaged-English dictionary, by John F. Mager." *Language*, 31 (1955), 163-165.

——, "The organization of language : a stratificational view," *Georgetown Monograph Series*, No. 17 (1964), 65-95.

——, "What is a dictionary?" Paper given to the Conference on Lexicography, LSA, Columbus, Ohio, July 23, 1970.

Goodenough, Ward H. "Componential analysis," *Science*, 156 (1967), 1203-1209.

——, "Componential analysis and the study of meaning," *Language*, 32 (1956), 195-216.

Gove, Philip B. "The history of 'dord'," *American Speech*, 29 (1954), 136-138.

——, "Linguistic advances and lexicography," *Word Study* (Oct. 1961), 3-8. (= Sledd and Ebbitt 1962 : 65-74).

——, "The nonlexical and the encyclopedic," *Names*, 13 (1965), 103-115.

——, "On defining adjectives : part I," *American Speech*, 43 (1968), 5-32.

——, "Repetition in defining," *College Composition and Communication*, 16 (1965), 231-236. (= Gove 1967:9-13).

——, (ed.). *The Role of the Dictionary* (Indianapolis : Bobbs-Merrill Co., 1967.)

——, "Subject orientation within the definition," *Monograph Series on Languages and Linguistics*, 14 (1961), 95-107.

——, "Usage in the dictionary," *College English*, 27 (1966), 285-292.

Greenberg, Joseph H. *Universals of Language* (Cambridge, Mass. : The MIT Press, 1963.)

Gropper, George L. "Why is a picture worth a thousand words?" *A V Communication Review*, Vol. 11, No. 4 (1963), 75-95.

Guilbert, Louis. "Le dictionnaire du français contemporain," *Cahiers de Lexicologie*, 1 (1967), 115-119.
——, *Le Lexique—Langue Française*, 2 (1969).
Haas, Mary R. "What belongs in a bilingual dictionary?" in Householder and Saporta, 45-50.
Haas, William. "The theory of translation," *Philosophy*, 37 (1962), 208-228.
Hall, Robert A., Jr. "Review of diccionario critico etimológico de la langua castellana, by J. Corminas," *Language*, 39 (1963), 116-125.
——, "Some recent developments in American linguistics," *Neuphilologisches Mitteilungen*, 70 (1969), 192-227.
Halliday, M. A. K., Angus McIntosh, and Peter Strevens. *The Linguistic Sciences and Language Teaching*.(Bloomington : Indiana University Press, 1965) First published in 1964.
Hammel, E. A. (ed.) *Formal Semantic Analysis, American Anthropologist*, 67/5 pt 2 (Menasha, Wis., 1965).
Harrell, Richard S. "Some notes on bilingual lexicography," in Householder and Saporta, 51-61.
Haskel, Peggy Irene. "Collections as a measure of stylistic variety," Paper presented to the symposium for literary and linguistic uses of the computer, Cambridge University, March 24-26 (1970).
Hattori, R. S. "The analysis of meaning," in *For Roman Jakobson*, ed. by Morris Halle (The Hague : Mouton, 1956), 207-212.
Haugen, Einar. "Review of Svensk-Engelsk fackordbok for naringsliv, forvaltning, undervisning och forskning," *Language*, 43 (1967), 561-564.
——, "The semantics of Icelandic orientation," *Word*, 13 (1957), 447-459.
Hayakawa, S. I. *Language in Thought and Action* (New York : Harcourt, Brace and World, Inc., 1941).
Haywood, John A. *Arabic Lexicography* (Leiden : E. J. Brill, 1960).
Heny, Frank W. "Lexical classes and semantic universals," Presented at the LSA meeting, 1968.
Hietsch, Otto. "Meaning discrimination in modern lexicography," *Modern Language Journal*, XLII (1958), 232-234.
Hill, Archibald A. "Correctness and style in English composition," *College English*, 12 (1951), pp. 280-285. Reprinted in *A Linguistic Reader*, ed. by Graham Wilson (New York : Harper & Row, 1967), 49-56.
——, "Grammaticality," *Word*, 17 (1961), 1-10.
——, *Introduction to Linguistic Structures* (New York : Harcourt, Brace & World, 1958.)
——, "Laymen, lexicographers, and linguists," *Language* 46 (1970), 245-258.
——, "Linguistic principles for interpreting meaning," *College English*, 22 (1961), 466-473.
—— (ed.), *Linguistics Today* (New York : Basic Books, Inc., 1969).
——, "A note on primitive languages," *International Journal of American Linguistics*, 18 (1952), 172-177.
——, *Oral Approach to English*, 2 vol. (Tokyo : The English Langue Education Council, Inc., 1965 & 1966).
——, "Principles governing semantic parallels," *Studies in Literature and Language*, 1 (1959), 356-365.
——, "The promises and limitations of the newest type of grammatical analysis," *TESOL Quarterly*, 1 (1966), 319-337.
——, "A re-examination of the English articles," *17th Annual Round Table*, ed. by F. P. Dinneen, S. J., No. 19 (Georgetown University, 1966), 217-231.
——, "Review of An Introduction to General Linguistics by Francis P. Dinneen," *Lingua*, 22 (1969), 237-244.

——, "Review of Dictionaries and That Dictionary by Sledd and Ebbitt," *Roundtable of the South Central College English Association*, 4 (1963), 2.

——, "Some thoughts on segmentation of lexical meaning," presented at the International Conference on Lexicography in New York, June 1972.

——, "Testing a dictionary" *Virginia Quarterly Review*, 28 (1952), pp. 131-135.

——, "The typology of writing systems," in *Papers in Linguistics in Honor of Léon Dostert*, ed. by William M. Austin (The Hague : Mouton, 1967), 92-99.

——, "The use of dictionaries in language teaching," *Language Learning*, 1 (1948), 9-13.

Hiorth, Finngeir. "Arrangement of meanings in lexicography," *Lingua*, 4 (1955), 413-424.

Hockett, Charles. *A Course in Modern Linguistics* (New York : Macmillan, 1958).

——, "Linguistic elements and their relations," *Language*, 37 (1961), 29-53.

Hoenigswald, Henry M. "Lexicography and grammar," in Householder and Saporta, 103-110.

Hoffer, Bates L., III. *Linguistic Principles in Lexicography* (Unpublished Ph.D. thesis, University of Texas at Austin, 1967.)

Hoijer, Harry, (ed.) *Language in Culture* (Chicago : University of Chicago Press, 1954).

Householder, Fred W. "On the uniqueness of semantic mapping," *Word*, 18 (1962), 173-185.

——, and Sol Saporta, eds. *Problems in Lexicography* (Bloomington : Indiana University, 1967).

Hulbert, James Root. *Dictionaries : British and American* (Tonbridge Kent : Andre Deutsch Ltd., 1955.)

Iannucci, James E. "Explanatory matters in bilingual dictionaries," *Babel*, V (1959), 195-199.

——, "Meaning discrimination in bilingual dictionaries," in Householder and Saporta, 201-216.

——, "Meaning discrimination in bilingual dictionaries : a new lexicographical technique," *Modern Language Journal*, XLI (1957), 272-281, and XLII (1958), 232-234.

——, "Review of New Revised Velazquez Spanish and English Dictionary, New York, 1959" *Hispania*, XLIII (1960), 138.

Imbs, P. "Au seuil de la lexicographie," *Cahiers de Lexicologie*, II (1960), 3-17.

Iordan, I. "Principes de la définition dans les dictionnaires unilingues," *Mélanges Ling.*, Bucarest, 1957, pp. 223-234.

Jackendoff, Ray. "Morphological and semantic regularities in the lexicon," *Language* 51 (1975), 639-671.

Jacobs, Jane, "Dictionary making in the United States," *Neuphilologische Mitteilungen*, LI (1950), pp. 145-51.

Jacobs, Roderick A. and Rosenbaum, Peter S. (eds.) *Readings in English Transformational Grammar*, (Waltham, Massachusetts : Ginn and Company, 1970).

Jakobson, Roman. "On linguistic aspects of translation," in *On Translation*, ed. by Reuben A. Brower (Cambridge, Mass. : Harvard University Press, 1959.)

Joos, Martin. "Cryptography in literate media," presented at the International Conference on Lexicography in New York, June, 1972.

——, (ed.). *Readings in Linguistics* (Washington : The Graphic Arts Press, 1957).

——, "Review of A Glossary of American Technical Linguistic Usage 1925-1950, by Eric P. Hamp," *Language*, 34 (1958), 279-288.

——, "Semology : a linguistic theory of meaning," *Studies in Linguistics*, 13 (1958), 53-70.

——, "Structure in meaning," *Georgetown Monograph Series*, No. 13 (1960), 41-48.

Josselson, H. "Automatization of lexicography," *Cahiers de Lexicologie*, IX (1966), 73-87.

——, "Lexicography and the computer," in *To Honour Roman Jakobson*, II (The Hague : Mouton, 1967.)

Kahane, Henry and Renée. "Problems in modern Greek lexicography," in Householder and Saporta, 249-262.

Kandler, Günther. "On the problem of quality in translation : basic considerations," in *Quality in Translation*, ed. by C. Cary and R. W. Jumpelt (New York : The Macmillan Co., 1963), 291-298.

Katre, Sumitra Mangesh. *Lexicography* (Annamalainger, Madras : Annamalai University, 1965).

Katz, Jerrold J. "Mentalism in linguistics," *Language*, 40 (1964), 124-137.

——, *The Philosophy of Language* (New York : Harper and Row, 1966).

——, "Recent issues in semantic theory," *Foundations of Language*, 3 (1967), 124-194.

——, and Jerry A. Fodor. "The structure of a semantic theory," *Language*, 39 (1963), 170-210. [= *Structure of Language*, ed. by Fodor and Katz (Englewood Cliffs: Prentice-Hall, 1964), 479-518.]

Keller, Howard H. "Review of Russian Derivational Dictionary by Dean S. Worth, Andrew S. Kozak, and Donald B. Johnson," *Language*, 48 (1972), 197-200.

Kilburn, Patrick E. "The gentleman's guide to linguistic etiquette," *Union College Symposium*, 9 (1970), 2-6.

Knudson, T., and Sommerfelt, A. "Principles of unilingual dictionary definitions," in *Proceedings of the Eighth International Congress of Linguists* ed. by E. Siversten (Oslo : Oslo University Press, 1958), 92-98.

Kohl, Marvin. "Ought God be in Webster's Third?" *Names*, 16 (1968), 134-135.

Korzybski, Alfred. *Science and Sanity : an introduction to non-Aristotelian systems and general semantics* (Lancaster, Pa. : Science Pres, for International Non-Aristotelian Library Publishing Co., 1933.)

Krapp, George Philip. *The English Language in America*, Vol. 1 (New York : The Century Company, 1925), pp. 351-377.

Kroeber, A. L. "Semantic contribution of lexicostatistics," *International Journal of American Linguistics*, 27 (1961), 1-8.

Kučera, Henry. "Computers in language analysis and in lexicography," in *The American Heritage Dictionary of the English Language*, ed. by William Morris (New York : American Heritage and Houghton Mifflin, 1969), xxxviii-xi.

——, and W. Nelson Francis. *Computational Analysis of Present-day American English*. (Providence, R. I. : Brown University Press, 1967.)

Kurath, Hans. "The semantic patterning of words." *Monograph Series on Languages and Linguistics*, 14 (1961), 91-94.

Labov, William. "The study of language in its social context," *Studium Generale*, 23 (1970), 30-87.

Laffal, Julius. *Pathological and Normal Language* (New York : Atherton Press, 1965).

Lamb, Sydney M. "The nature of the machine translation problem," *Journal of Verbal Learning and Verbal Behavior*, 4 (1965), 196-210.

——, *Outline of Stratificational Grammar* (Washington : Georgetown University Press, 1966).

Laurie, S. S. *John Amos Comenius : His Life and Educational Works* (Cambridge : the University Press, 1904).

Lees, R. B. "On very deep grammatical structure," in *Readings in English Transformational Grammar*, ed. by Peter S. Rosenbaum (Waltham, Mass. : Ginn and Company, 1970), 134-144.

Legman, G. "On sexual speech and slang," Introduction to *Dictionary of Slang and its Analogues*, by W. E. Henley (New Hyde Park, N.Y. : University Books, 1966), I. xxx-xciv.

Lehmann, W. P. "Review of two etymological dictionaries," *College English*, 28 (1967), 626-628.

Leont'ev, A. A. "The concept of the formal grammatical word," *Linguistics*, 15 (1965), 33-39.

Lepschy, G. C. "Problems of semantics," *Linguistics*, 15 (1965), 40-65.

Lightner, Theodore. "Review of 'Dictionnaire inverse de la langue française' by Alphonse Juilland," *Language*, 51 (1975), 210-211.

Linker, Jerry Mac. *The Interaction of Cognitive Factors, Visual Fidelity, and Learning Tasks in Learning from Pictures* (Unpublished Ph.D. Thesis, University of Texas at Austin, 1971.)

Ljudskanov, Alexandre. *Traduction Humaine et Traduction Mécanique.* (Paris : Association Jean-Favard pour le développement de la linguistique quantitative, 1969.)

Lorge, Irving. "The English semantic count," *Teachers College Record*, 39 (1937), 65-77.

Lounsbury, Floyd G. "A semantic analysis of the Pawnee kinship usage," *Language*, 32 (1956), 158-194.

——, "The structural analysis of kinship semantics," *Proceedings of the International Congress of Linguists*, 8 (1964), 1073-1093.

MacKey, William Francis. *Language Teaching Analysis* (Bloomington : Indiana University Press, 1967).

Maclay, Howard. "Linguistics overview," in *Semantics*, ed. by Danny D. Steinberg and Leon A. Jakobovits (Cambridge : Cambridge University Press, 1971), 157-182.

Madkūr, Ibrāhīm. *Fi 'l-Lughati wa 'l-Adab* (Cairo: Dāru 'l-Ma'ārif, 1971).

Malkiel, Yakov. "Distinctive features in lexicography: a typological approach to dictionaries exemplified in Spanish," *Romance Philology*, 12 (1959), 366-399, 13: 111-155.

——, "Lexicography," in *The Learning of Language* ed. by Carroll E. Reed (New York : Appleton-Century-Crofts, 1971), 363-387.

——, "Review of Thesaurus Praeromanicus," *Language* 47 (1971) 465-487.

——, "A typological classification of dictionaries on the basis of distinctive features," in Householder and Saporta, 3-24.

Malone, Kemp. "On defining mahogany," *Language*, 16 (1940), 308-318.

——, "Structural linguistics and bilingual dictionaries," in Householder and Saporta, 111-118.

March, Francis A. "Whitney's influence on the study of modern languages and lexicography," in *The Whitney Memorial Meeting*, ed. by Charles R. Lanman (Boston : Ginn and Co., 1897), 29-36.

Marchand, Hans. *The Categories and Types of Present-day English Word-formation* (München : Verlag C.H. Beck, 1969).

Marckwardt, Albert H. "Whither the desk dictionary?" *Language Learning*, 2/1 (1949), 25-29.

——, "Dictionaries and the English Language," *English Journal* 52 (1963), 336-345. (= Gove 1967: 31-38).

——, "The new Webster dictionary: a critical appraisal," in *Reading in Applied English Linguistics*, ed. by Harold B. Allen (New York : Appleton-Century-Crofts, 1964), 476-485. 2nd. ed.

Marcus, S. "Définitions logiques et définitions lexicographiques," *Langages*, No. 19 (Sept, 1970), 87-91.

Martin, Samuel E. "Selection and presentation of ready equivalents in a translation dictionary," in Householder and Saporta, 153-159.

Mathews, Mitford M. "The freshman and his dictionary," *College Composition and Communication*, 6 (1955), 187-190. Reprinted in *Readings in Applied English Linguistics*, ed. by Harrold B. Allen (New York : Appleton-Century-Crofts, 1958), 434-439.

——, "The largest English dictionaries," in *Words: How to Know Them*, ed. by M. M. Mathews (New York: Holt, Rinehart & Winston, Inc., 1956) pp. 1-9. Reprinted in James Sledd and Wilma Ebbitt (eds.) *Dictionaries & That Dictionary* pp. 21-28.

——, "Problems encountered in preparation of a dictionary of American words and meanings," in *English Institute Essays* (New York: Columbia University Press, 1947), 76-96.

——, *A Survey of English Dictionaries* (New York: Russell & Russell, 1966)—first published in 1933.

Mathiot, Madeleine. "The place of the dictionary in linguistic description," *Language*, 43 (1967), 703-724.

Matoré, G. *Histoire des Dictionnaires Français* (Paris: Larousse, 1968).

McCawley, James D. "Meaning and the description of languages," *Kotoba no Uchu*, Vol. 2 (1967) nos. 9 (10-18), 10 (38-48), 11 (51-57).

——, "The role of semantics in a grammar," in *Universals in Linguistic Theory*, ed. by Emmon Bach and Robert T. Harms (New York: Holt, Rinehart and Winston, Inc., 1968), 125-170.

——, "Interpretative semantics meets Frankenstein," *Foundations of Language*, 7 (1971), 285-296.

McDavid, Raven I., Jr. "Some principles for American dialect study," *Studies in Linguistics*, 1/12 (1942), 1-11.

——, "The Merriam Third: self-inflicted wounds?" Presented to the Present-Day English section (English 13), MLA (1966).

——, "Dialect labels in the Merriam Third," *Publications of the American Dialect Society*, 47 (1967), 1-22.

McIntosh, Angus, and M. A. K. Halliday. *Patterns of Language* (Bloomington: Indiana University Press, 1967)—first published in 1966.

McMillan, James B. "Five college dictionaries," *College English*, 10 (1949), 214-221.

Meyers, Russell. "The nervous system and general semantics: II. 'reality' and 'unreality'." *ETC*, 6 (1948), 27-38.

Mitterand, H. "Deux dictionnaires français: Le Petit Robert et Le Dictionnaire du Français Contemporain," *Le Français dans le Monde*, No. 59, (1968), 24-29.

Morris, Charles. *Foundations of the Theory of Signs* (International encyclopedia of unified science, 1.2) (Chicago Press, 1938).

——, *Signs, Language and Behavior* (New York: Prentice-Hall, 1946.)

Morris, William. "The making of a dictionary," *College Composition and Communication*, 20 (1969), 198-203.

Mower, Morris Leon & Le Roy, Barney. "Which are the most important dictionary skills?" *Elementary English*, 45 (1968), 468-471.

Murray, J. A. H. *The Evolution of English Lexicography* (Oxford: The Clarendon Press, 1900.)

Nassār, Hussein. *Al-Mu'jam Al-'arabī* (Cairo: Dāru 'l-Kātib, 1956.)

Newman, John B. "The semantic analysis of ordinary language," *The Quarterly Journal of Speech*, 49 (1963), 410-416.

Nida, Eugene A. "Analysis of meaning and dictionary making," *International Journal of American Linguistics*, 24 (1958), 279-292.

——, *Bible Translating: An Analysis of Principles and Procedures* (New York: American Bible Society, 1947.)

——, "Linguistics and semantic structure," in *Studies in Languages and Linguistics in Honor of Charles C. Fries*, ed. by Albert H. Marckwardt (Ann Arbor: English Language Institute, 1964.)

——, "Some problems of semantic structure and translational equivalence," in *William Cameron Townsend en el XXV aniversario del I.L.V.*, (Mexico, 1958), 313-325.

——, "A system for the description of semantic elements," *Word*, 7 (1951), 1-14.

——, *Toward a Science of Translating* (Leiden : E. J. Brill, 1964).

Noble, C. E. "An analysis of meaning," *Psychological Review*, 59 (1952), 421-430.

Oettinger, Anthony G. *Automatic Language Translation*. Harvard Monographs in Applied science No. 8 (Cambridge, Mass. : Harvard University Press, 1960.)

Olmsted, David L., and O. K. Moore. "Language, psychology and linguistics," *Psychological Review*, 59. 414-420.

O'Neil, Wayne. "The spelling and pronounciation of English," in *The American Heritage Dictionary of the English Language*, ed. by William Morris (Boston : American Heritage Publishing Co., Inc., 1969). xxxv-xxxvii.

Osgood, Charles E. "The nature and measurement of meaning," *Psychological Bulletin*, 49 (1952), 197-237.

——, George J. Suci, and Percy H. Tannenbaum. *The Measurement of Meaning* (Urbana, Ill. : University of Illinois Press, 1957).

Painter, J. A. "Implications of the Cornell concordances for computing," in *Literary Data Processing Conference Proceedings* (IBM Corporation, 1964), 160-170.

Papp, F. "Traitement automatique de la composante sémantique du dictionnaire," *Traduction Automatique*, Symposium international des pays membres du COMECON, (10-13 Octobre, 1967), 1-15.

Pike, Kenneth L. "A guide to publications related to tagmemic theory," *CTL*, 3 (1966), 365-394.

——, *Language in Relation to a Unified Theory of the Structure of Human Behavior* (The Hague : Mouton, 1967).

——, "A training device for translation theory and practice," *Bibliotheca Sacra*, 114 (1957), 347-362.

Pimsleur, Paul. "Semantic frequency counts," *Mechanical Translation*, 4 (1957), 11-13.

Pollock, Thomas Clark. "A theory of meaning analyzed," *General Semantics Monographs*, 3 (1942), 1-25.

Pooley, Robert C. "Dictionaries and language change," *Language, Linguistics, and School Programs, Proceedings of the Spring Institutes, 1963*. (Champaign, Ill., NCTE, 1963.)

Pos, H. J. "The foundation of word-meanings, different approaches," *Lingua*, 1 (1948), 281-291.

Pottier, B. "La définition sémantique dans les dictionnaires." *Travaux de Ling. et de Littér.*, III (1965), 33-39.

——, "Champ sémantique, champ d'expérience et structure lexicale," in *Probleme der Semantik* ed. by T. Elwert (Wiesbaden, 1968), 37-40.

Pyles, Thomas. "Dictionaries and usage," in *Linguistics Today*, ed. by Archibald A. Hill (New York : Basic Books, Inc., Publishers, 1969), 127-136.

Quemada, B. *Les dictionnaires du français moderne, 1539-1863, étude sur leur histoire, leur types et leur méthodes.* (Paris : Didier, 1968).

Quine, Willard V. "The problem of meaning in linguistics," in *The Structure of Language : Readings in the Philosophy of Language*, ed. by J. A. Fodor and J. J. Katz (Englewood Cliffs, N.J. : Prentice-Hall, 1961), 21-32.

Ramsay, Robert L. "Taking the census of English words," *American Speech*, 8/1 (1933), 36-41.

Razran, Gregory. "A quantitative study of meaning by a conditioned salivary technique (semantic conditioning)," *Science*, 90 (1939), 89-90.

Read, Allen Walker. "Approaches to lexicography and semantics," in *Current Trends in Linguistics*, ed. Thomas A. Sebeok, Volume 10, *Linguistics in North America* (The Hague : Mouton, 1972).

——, "A discrimination among synonyms of the word 'meaning'," *Monograph Series on Languages and Linguistics*, 8 (1955), 123-133.

——, "The scope of the American dictionary," *American Speech*, 8/3 (1933), 10-20.

——, "The lexicographer and general semantics, with a plan for a 'semantic guide to current English'," *General Semantics Monographs*, 3 (1942), 37-46.

——, "An account of the word 'semantics'," *Word*, 4 (1948), 78-97.

——, "English words with constituent elements having independent semantic value," *Philologica: the Malone anniversary studies*, ed. by T. A. Kirby and H. B. Woolf (Baltimore: Johns Hopkins Press, 1949), 306-312.

——, "That dictionary or the dictionary?" *Consumer Reports*, 28 (1963), 488-492.

——, "Desk dictionaries," *Consumer Reports* 28 (1963), 547-550.

——, "A dictionary of the English of England: problems and findings," Presented to the Present-Day English section (English 13), MLA, December 27 (1968). mimeographed.

——, "The labeling of national and regional variation in popular dictionaries," in Householder and Saporta, 217-227.

Rey, A. "Les dictionnaires, forme et contenu," *Cahiers de Lexicologie*, II (1965), 66-102.

——, "Dictionnaire de la langue française d'Émile Littré, abrégé par A. Beaujean, révision et mise à jour sous la direction de G. Venzac," *Zeitschrift für Romanische Philologie*, 83 (1968), 55-72.

——, "Typologie génétique des dictionnaires," *Langages*, No. 19 (Sept. 1970), 48-68.

——, *La Lexicologie: Lectures* (Paris: Librairie C. Klincksieck, 11 Rue de Lille, Paris VIIe, 1970).

Rey-Debove, J. (ed.). *La Lexicographie* (Paris: Didier/Larousse, 1970).

——, "Le domaine du dictionnaire," *Langages*, No. 19 (Sept. 1970), 3-34.

Rivers, Wilga M. *The Psychologist and the Foreign Language Teacher* (Chicago: The University of Chicago Press, 1964.)

Robinson, Dow F. *Manual for Bilingual Dictionaries*. 3 vols. (Santa Ana, Cal.: Summer Institute of Linguistics, 1969.)

Sampson, Geoffrey. "Is there a universal phonetic alphabet?", *Language*, 50 (1974), 236-259.

Sapir, Edward. "The status of linguistics as a science," *Language*, 5 (1929), 207-214.

Saporta, Sol. (ed.). *Psycholinguistics: a book of readings* (New York: Holt, Rinehart and Winston, 1961).

——, "Review of Questions of Meanings by László Antal," *Word*, 20 (1964), 282-283.

Saussure, F. de. *Cours de linguistique générale* (Paris: Payot, 1949).

Schwietering, J. "On dictionary-making," *German Life and Letters*, 4 (1950), 176-182.

Sebeok, Thomas A. "Materials for a typology of dictionaries," *Lingua*, 11 (1962), 363-374.

——, "Review of K. Nielsen and A. Nesheim, *Lapp Dictionary*," *American Anthropologist*, 59 (1957), 1133.

Sedelow, Sally Yeates. "The computer in the humanities and fine arts," *Computing Surveys*, 2 (1970), 89-110.

Sell, Lewis L. *Practical Polyglot Technical Lexicography and the Professional Polyglot Technician*. (New York: S. F. Vanni, 1943.)

Sledd, James. "Breaking, umlaut, and the southern drawl," *Language*, 42 (1966), 18-41. Reprinted in *English Linguistics*, ed. by Harold Hungerford, Jay Robinson, and James Sledd (Glenview, Ill.: Scott, Foresman and Co., 1970), 244-273.

——, "Dollars and dictionaries: the limits of commercial lexicography," in *New Aspects of Lexicography: Literary Criticism, Intellectual History, and Social Change*, ed. by Howard D. Weinbot (Carbondale, Ill.: Southern Illinois University Press, 1971).

——, and Ebbitt, Wilma R. (eds.) *Dictionaries and that Dictionary*, (Chicago: Scott, Foresman, 1962).

——, and Gwin J. Kolb. *Dr. Johnson's Dictionary: Essays in the Biography of a Book.* (Chicago : The University of Chicago Press, 1955.)

Smith, Henry Lee, Jr. "Dialects of English," in *The American Heritage Dictionary of the English Language*, ed. by William Morris (Boston; American Heritage Publishing Co., Ind., 1969.) xxv-xxx.

——, "The modalities of human communication," *General Semantics Bulletin*, 32-33 (1965), 6-17.

Smith, Karl U. "The scientific principles of textbook design and illustration," *A V Communication Review*, 8 (1960), 27-49.

Sommerfelt, A. "Sémantique et lexicographie. Remarques sur la tâche du lexicographie," in *Diachronic and Synchronic Aspects of Language*, ed. by A. Sommerfelt (The Hague : Mouton and Co., 1962), 273-276.

Sonkin, Robert. "Alexander Bryan Johnson's plan for a 'collated dictionary'," *Language and Value*, ed. by Charles L. Todd and Russell T. Blackwood, (New York : Greenwood Publishing Corporation, 1969), 90-121.

Spaulding, Seth. "Communication potential of pictorial illustration," *A V Communication Review*, 4 (1956), 31-46.

——, "Research on pictorial illustration," *A V Communication Review*, 3 (1955), 35-45.

Sperber, Hans. A co-operative research project on a dictionary of political words and phrases. (Columbus, Ohio : Graduate School, Ohio State University, 1945).

Stachowitz, Rolf A. "The construction and application of a computerized dictionary," Presented to the Conference on Lexicography, LSA, Columbus, Ohio, July 23, 1970. [photoprinted.]

Starnes, De Witt T. *Robert Estienne's Influence on Lexicography.* (Austin : University of Texas Press, 1963.)

——, and Noyes, Gertrude E. *The English Dictionary From Cawdrey to Johnson 1604-1755.* (Chapel Hill : The University of North Carolina Press, 1946.)

Steger, Stewart Archer. *American Dictionaries* (Baltimore, 1913).

Steinberg, Danny D. and Jakobovits, Leon A., ed. *Semantics* (Cambridge : The University Press, 1971.)

Stern, G. *Meaning and the Change of Meaning* (Indiana : Indiana University Press, 1964), 1st ed. 1931.

Story, George M. *A Newfoundland Dialect Dictionary: A Survey of the Problems.* (St. John's, Newfoundland : Memorial University, 1956.)

Swanson, Donald C. "The selection of entries for a bilingual dictionary," in Householder and Saporta, 63-77.

Thomas, Charles R. *Data Element Dictionary: Facilities.* Preliminary Draft (Western Interstate Commission for Higher Education, Boulder, Colo. 1969.)

Tietze, Andreas. "Problems of Turkish lexicography," in Householder and Saporta, 263-272.

Trager, George L. "The systematization of the Whorf hypothesis," *Anthropological Linguistics*, I, (1959), 31-35.

Twaddell, W. Freeman. "Meanings, habits and rules," *Language Learning*, 2/1 (1949), 4-11.

Twyford, L. C. "Educational communications media," in *The Encyclopedia of Educational Research*, 4th edition, ed. by R. L. Ebel. (Boston : The Macmillan Company, 1969), 367-379.

Ullmann, S. *Semantics* (New York : Barnes and Noble, Inc., 1962.)

Ulvestad, Bjarne. "Review of Norwegian-English Dictionary, ed. by Einar Haugen," *Language*, 44 (1968), 378-388.

Unbegaun, Boris O. "Soviet lexicology in the sixties," *Monograph Series on Languages and Linguistics*, 24 (1971), 259-267.

UNESCO. *Guidelines for the Establishment and Development of Monolingual Scientific and Technical Thesauri for Information Retrieval* (Paris : UNESCO, 1970.)

Urdang, Laurence. "Review of Manual of Lexicography by Ladislav Zgusta et al." *Language*, 51 (1975), 220-230.

——, "Review of Problems in Lexicography," *Language*, 39 (1963), 586-94.

——, "The systems designs and devices used to process The Random House Dictionary of the English Language," *Computers and Humanities*, 1 (1966), 31-33.

——, "The use of typographic coding in information retrieval," *Proceedings of the American Documentation Institute*, Oct. 3-7 (1966), 193-200.

Vendler, Zeno. *Linguistics in Philosophy* (Ithaca, N.Y. : Cornell University Press, 1967.)

Vizetelly, Frank H. *The Development of the Dictionary of the English Language* (New York : Funk & Wagnalls Co., 1915.)

——, "The ideal dictionary," *American Speech*, 1 (1926), 275-281.

Voegelin, C. F. "Review of Vocabulario Tarahumara, by K. Simon Hilton et al.," *American Anthropologist*, 63 (1961), 876-878.

Wallace, Anthony R. C., and John Atkins. "The meaning of kinship terms," *American Anthropologist*, 62 (1960), 58-80.

Walsh, S. Padraig (Comp.) *English Language Dictionaries in Print : A Comparative Analysis* (Newark, Delaware : Reference Books Research Publications, Inc., 1965.)

Warfel, Harry R. "Dictionaries and linguistics," *College English*, 22 (1961), 473-478.

Weekley, E. "On dictionaries," *Atlantic Monthly*, (June 1924), 782-791. (= Sledd and Ebbitt, pp. 9-21.)

Weinbrot, Howard D. ed. *New Aspects of Lexicography : Literary Criticism, Intellectual History, and Social Change.* (Carbondale, Ill. : Southern Illinois University Press, 1971.)

Weinreich, Uriel. "Explorations in semantic theory," *Current Trends in Linguistics 3*, ed. by Thomas A. Sebeok (The Hague : Mouton, 1966), 395-447.

——, "Lexicographic definition in descriptive semantics," in Householder and Saporta, 25-44.

——, "Lexicology," *Current Trends in Linguistics, Vol. 1.* ed. by Thomas A. Sebeok (The Hague : Mouton, 1963), 60-93.

——, "On the semantic structure of language," in *Universals in Language*, ed. by Joseph H. Greenberg (Cambridge, Mass. : M.I.T. Press, 1963), 114-171.

——, "Travels through semantic space," *Word*, 14 (1958), 346-366.

——, "Webster's Third : a critique of its semantics," *International Journal of American Linguistics*, 30 (1964), 405-409.

Wells, Rulon. "Meaning and use," *Word*, 10 (1954), 235-250.

Wentworth, Harold. "Words in use," *Saturday Review of Literature*, 8 (August 15, 1931), 62.

West, Michael. *Definition Vocabulary* (Toronto : The University of Toronto Press, 1935.)

White, J. H. "The methodology of sememic analysis with special application to the English preposition," *Mechanical Translation*, (August, 1964), 15-31.

Whitney, William D. *Language and the Study of Language : Twelve Lectures on the Principles of Linguistic Science.* (New York : Scribner, Armstrong & Co., 1876.)

Whorf, Benjamin Lee. *Language, Thought, and Reality*, ed. by John B. Carroll (Cambridge, Mass. : M.I.T. Press, 1956.)

Williams, Edwin B. "Analysis of the problem of meaning discrimination in Spanish and English bilingual lexicography," *Babel : Revue International de la Traduction*, 6 (1960), 121-125.

——, "The problems of bilingual lexicography particularly as applied to Spanish and English," *Hispanic Review*, xxvii (1959), 246-253.

Yorkey, Richard. "Which desk dictionary is best for foreign students of English?" *TESOL Quarterly*, 3 (1969), 257-270.

Zawadowski, L. "La polysémie prétendue," *Bulletin de la Société Polonaise de Linguistique*, 18 (1959), 11-48.

——, "La signification des morphèmes polysèmes," *Bulletin de la Société Polonaise de Linguistique*, 17 (1958), 67-95.

Zgusta, Ladislav. "Equivalents and explanations in bilingual dictionaires," Presented to the Conference on Lexicography, LSA, Columbus, Ohio, July 23, 1970, mimeographed.

——, "Idle thoughts of an idle fellow, or diversions of MT lexicography," a mimeographed paper. Linguistic Research Center, The University of Texas at Austin, 1971.

—— et al. *Manual of Lexicography* [Janua linguarum, series maior, 39.], (Prague : Academia, Publishing House of the Czechoslovak Academy of Sciences; The Hague & Paris : Mouton, 1971.)

Ziff, Paul. *Semantic Analysis* (Ithaca, New York : Cornell University Press, 1960.)

INDEX

adjectives 55-56, 65, 71, 99
adverbs 57, 99
American lexicography 2
appendices 111-112
Arabic lexicography 2, 8, 89, 90, 92
arrangement of entries, see entries 41, 95,
  105

Ba'albaki, Munir 41, 95, 105
Barnhart, C.L. 3, 19, 35, 36, 80, 86, 93,
  95, 105
Bishop, Morris 88
Blachère, Regis 76
Bloch, Bernard 37, 38, 39
Bloomfield, Leonard 32, 33, 39, 51
Bluteau 89
Bolinger, Dwight L. 7, 9, 55
borrowing, word 61-62
Bronstein, Arthur J. 45
Brown, Labota L. 7
Bull, William E. 61

case government 56
categories, grammatical 63, 64
Catford, J.C. 59, 65, 103
Chomsky, Noam 7, 32
circularity 79
citations 89-89; see also illustrative examples
clarity 102
classification of dictionaries 12-31
  Al-Kasimi's, 17-31, Malkiel's, 14-16,
  Sebeok's, 13-14, Shcherba's, 12-13,
  Rey's, 16-17
coinage 61
Coleridge, S.T. 3
colloquial 87-88
Comenius, John Amos 96
commercial lexicography 3
compactness 100-101
comparison 55
completeness 102
compounding, word 61
comprehension, dictionary for 24-26, 68-75
commercial lexicography 3
commutation test 59-60
concordance 12, 13
connotations 15, 64

contextual examples, see illustrative exam
  ples 15, 64
context words or phrases 71
contrastive analysis 38, 49
Cornyn, William S. 17
correctness 84-85
Craigie, W.A. 28
cross reference 14, 52, 77
culture 62, 67, 92

De Camp, David 85
definitions 70, 106
  truncated 78-81
derivation 50
dialect, definition of 45-46
  recording – in dictionary 45-48
dialectal 88
dictionary
  abridged 29
  abstracted and generated 13-14
  bidirectional 26, 45, 72, 74
  bilingual 15, etc.
  computerized 26
  criteria for 109-112
  defining 13
  definition of 1, 4, 32
  descriptive 27-29, 83-84, 85, 92
  diachronic 15
  didactic 27
  encyclopedic 17, 29-31, 34
  etymological 8, 105
  function of 19, 30, 34, 104-105
  general 31
  historical 13, 27-29, 95, 97
  lexical 29-31
  monolingual 15, 35-36, 58, 104, 106
  multilingual 15
  normative 12, 27
  period 28
  plurilingual 15
  prescriptive 27, 83-84
  pronouncing 34
  purpose of 18-31, 49, 95, 109
  quadrilingual 15
  review of 14, 28
  sources of 14, 28
  special 31
  synchronic 15